"The sovereignty of (that will no doubt c eternity. But while the subject is inexhaustible in its riches, there is much we can know and can hold with confidence. In *Behold Our Sovereign God*, Mitch Chase skillfully treads the path between too little and too much, between shying away from difficult topics and succumbing to fruitless speculation. Grounding every word in Scripture, with boldness, nuance and clarity, he explores the riches of God's sovereignty, leading the reader to wonder and from wonder to worship."

Tim Challies author of *The Next Story*, *The Discipline of Spiritual Discernment*, and *Sexual Detox*.

"As I read this book, four things came repeatedly to mind: it is refreshingly honest, ruthlessly biblical, pastorally sensitive, and above all else, altogether persuasive. If you are looking for a clear-headed, Christ-exalting introduction to the sovereignty of God, you can do no better than Mitch Chase's excellent book."

Sam Storms, Pastor of Preaching and Vision at Bridgeway Church in Oklahoma City, President of Enjoying God Ministries, and author of *Chosen For Life* and *The Singing God*.

"Mitch Chase loves the Lord and the Bible, and he can help you understand how God's love and sovereignty are joined together such that none can sever. Read this book with an open Bible and a humble heart, and prepare to be amazed anew at the mercies of God."

James M. Hamilton Jr., Professor of Biblical Theology at The Southern Baptist Theological Seminary, Preaching Pastor of Kenwood Baptist Church in Louisville, and author of *God's Glory in Salvation Through Judgment* and *Revelation: The Spirit Speaks to the Churches.*

"From the mind and heart of a fellow-traveler comes a winsome and biblically-faithful portrayal of the sovereignty of God. Like so many others, Mitch Chase himself struggled to understand and embrace God's revelation of himself in Scripture as sovereign over nature and nations, suffering and salvation. But in the end, he sees and presents with clarity and rich insight what the Bible says on these important aspects of God's sovereign rulership over all things. Readers will never feel "pushed" by this book to accept ideas they find difficult. Rather, they will feel a tender and warm-hearted drawing of them to gaze more carefully into some of the riches of God's own glorious self-revelation. For those struggling to make sense of issues related to divine sovereignty, Chase has provided a superb resource, indeed one of the best they could pick up and read."

Bruce Ware, Professor of Christian Theology at The Southern Baptist Theological Seminary, and author of *The Man Christ Jesus* and *God's Greater Glory.*

Behold Our Sovereign God

All Things From Him,
Through Him, and To Him

MITCHELL L. CHASE

First Printing 2012

ISBN-13: 978-1-935909-52-1
ISBN-10: 1935909525

For John Piper,

whose sermons and books
exalt the God who reigns
over all things for His glory

TABLE OF CONTENTS

Introduction

The Journey Then and Now

This book may be a short journey, but no one should underestimate the value of brief travel. I've driven long distances and sat for many hours on planes traveling to the other side of the world, but some short trips have changed my life. On the day I married Stacie, I traveled only thirty minutes to the church for the ceremony. When our first son Jensen was born, we lived less than an hour from the hospital.

Think bigger now. Imagine the impact of just five minutes in the Grand Canyon. In that brief time your soul would be exposed to the magnificence of creation, to sights that stagger the mind and fill you with glorious insignificance. You won't leave unchanged.

There may always be more to see, more wonder to take in, but brief exposure to majesty can leave you flat on your face. Just ask Isaiah.

This book is a disproportionate treatment of its subject: the doctrine of God's sovereignty. This doctrine requires the careful assessment of extensive biblical evidence, involving nuanced explanations that must speak to controversial and complex questions. This labor is necessary since God has not been silent on how he works in his world. But just because God reveals himself is no guarantee we will listen. When a king asserts his authority, a citizen may turn a deaf ear of denial.

The topic of divine sovereignty is broad. While we cannot cover every biblical text and question (ahem, *objection*), the fruit of our study will deal with the major passages and key issues.[1] More will remain to be seen, but the glimpse we get will, by God's grace, cast a vision of divine grandeur in the eyes of our hearts.

One Decade, One Doctrine

Simply put, God's sovereignty refers to his control or rule in his world.[2] Over the last ten years, this doctrine has consumed my thinking. At times it's felt like a thorn in my soul, a perpetual nuisance agitating me without relief. In

---

1   I have determined (pun intended) which passages are "major" and which issues are "key" by spending time in the literature related to this topic. Certain Bible passages seem to come to the fore over and over, and particular questions are posed repeatedly as objections.

2   Related to God's sovereignty is his *providence*, which refers to his meticulous guidance of things toward a goal. Providence is God's purposeful superintendence of the details in his creation. When this book speaks of God's sovereignty, then, the reader should understand it as the exercise of God's supreme rule over all things. God doesn't merely preside over his creation, he rules *providentially*.

other moments the doctrine has been a supernova of power and light.

In the rest of this introduction, I want to reflect on my journey with God's sovereignty and then give suggestions for reading the next five chapters.

The Struggle Begins

Growing up I don't remember thinking much about God's control in the world. As a kid I sang "He's Got the Whole World in His Hands" but only realized much later the truth of that title: he has his hands *in* the world, in the *events* therein, and in the *details* of what happens — even in my life.

As a teen I would have told you God was sovereign but been unable to explain what that meant. I believed he was good and could bring good from evil, but that was the peak of my reflection until graduating high school. Those are two good truths to know and are integral to what the rest of the Bible teaches about God's sovereign rule, but my understanding was still limited.

Ten years ago, when I first enrolled in college theology courses, my professors dragged all kinds of issues into the open, provoking many in-class and post-class discussions. *If God is in control of the world, why does so much evil remain unchecked? If God is sovereign over the entire salvation process, what remains of human freedom? Does history unfold according to our decisions or according to God's decrees? How do we handle the subject of predestination? Does God permit sin or even ordain it for mysterious purposes? If man truly has free will, can God violate it and still be considered loving? If God controls what happens in the world, doesn't that make us puppets without a say?*

The philosophical and theological problems seemed endless and overwhelming. I was surrounded by people who thought differently about these issues, people who insisted on God's meticulous rule of all things, and they frequently pointed me to Scriptures that left me perplexed — Scriptures that frankly I'd either never seen before or never gave serious attention to.

For example, when Job lost his children, he said the Lord *took* them away (Job 1:21b). Joseph told his family that God *intended* his suffering (Gen 50:20a). The psalmist declared that God *controlled* fire and hail, rain and wind (Ps 148:8). God claimed to be the *cause* of calamity as well as blessing (Isa 45:7), to decree *both* good and bad things (Lam 3:37-38). Disaster doesn't strike a city apart from God's *will* (Amos 3:6b). Jesus said people cannot come to him *unless* the Father draws them (John 6:44a). When some Gentiles responded to Paul's preaching, those who believed had already been *appointed* for eternal life (Acts 13:48).

If you remember your first impressions of such verses, then perhaps you felt what I did — uncomfortable. The more I discovered and read such passages, the more God's sovereignty frustrated me. The more I read them, the more I resisted and insisted on my free will and asked questions in response. *Isn't the devil the one behind all suffering? Shouldn't my will remain untouched by God? Doesn't God decree only what is good, not things like disaster and calamity?*

Duck, Dodge, and Deny

I adopted a simple strategy with difficult passages: duck, dodge, and deny. Glimpsing God's sovereignty from a distance was fine, but zooming in on certain details of Scripture left me perplexed. I maintained a vague notion of God's sovereignty, but even I wasn't clear on what that notion entailed!

When it came to tough texts, I convinced myself it didn't matter whether they were there or not. And like most bad ideas, my strategy wasn't successful. Trying not to think about certain texts or words (like those starting with "pre-") just made me think about them more.

Adding to the burden of new theological problems, I met some college students in a Christian bookstore who berated me for not seeing sovereignty in a certain way. They believed nothing in the world happened outside God's will, but their tone wasn't humble or kind. They were rude, belligerent, and completely turned me off to a fair hearing of the texts they were beating me with. *If this is what people who believe this are like, I don't want any part of that theology.*[3]

---

3   This experience is all too common. Perhaps you've met an "angry Calvinist" who seems merciless about God's mercy and ruthless about grace. The problem is with the person, though, not the theology. Rightly perceiving God's sovereign grace will humble the proud heart of man. Predestination is a sword that slays the dragon of pride—not at the knees but at the neck!

The summer after my first year of college, I served as a youth minister under a patient pastor, Sam Waltman. His view of God was massive, his attention to the Bible was careful and precise, and he valued the experience of wading through deep waters—he'd done some wading himself. Over several months I asked many questions, and he answered me from the Bible with empathy and the tale of his own journey. He was farther down the road than I was, but it was refreshing to meet a fellow traveler.

Despite the planted seeds of helpful conversations and providential relationships, my view of God's sovereignty remained largely unchanged during my college years. But isn't that the way seeds work? It may look like nothing is happening, but the surface of the ground doesn't tell the whole story. You have to look underneath.

Underneath the surface, my view of God was being challenged for the first time ever. It wasn't totally wrong, but some aspects needed correction, recalibration, and expansion. I had not incorporated certain verses into my understanding of divine sovereignty. My view of God wasn't informed by the whole counsel of God.

Classroom instruction, though, seemed only to muddy the waters. My college professors explained away strict views of predestination, and they cast aside any notion that God ordained all that happened in the world. God couldn't will whatever took place, especially since evil things happen. If he did, wouldn't that make him evil too?

The struggle was on, and it was fierce.

Rumblings of a Coming Shift

You never know when a class will change your life. I started seminary in 2005, and my first class was an exposition of Isaiah. The course was a threshold. It was as though the preceding college years were all preparation for this one semester. The professor was Jim Hamilton, and he exegeted and probed the entire text of Isaiah for five months. The teaching and discussion challenged my understanding of divine sovereignty, and I could feel a paradigm shift slowly taking place.

While I was still reluctant to embrace certain theological interpretations, it seemed the Bible wasn't giving me other options. I felt desperate to find compelling interpretations which would say something different than what the text naturally said, but in the end I was unconvinced by these alternatives.

I also read theologians on both sides of the debate so that I could understand different views held in church history. It became clear that the subject of sovereignty (especially in salvation) surfaced in past centuries and was not a recent controversy provoked by seminary students or their professors. The more questions I asked, the less sure I became about my presuppositions about how God worked in his world. The more texts I read, the more I felt like my world was falling apart.

Stacie and I were engaged during these months, and many Monday evenings after class I called her to vent my struggle with what I was reading, thinking, and learning.

She graciously received these late-night phone calls, talked at length with me about the issues, and we both realized how much larger the Bible's portrayal of God was than our own views. She was on the same journey on the same road. The longer the journey lasted, the clearer the truth became that this road was well-traveled by thousands (millions?) of past pilgrims. We were walking on their footprints, asking their questions, finding their answers, seeing what they saw.

Though at times I felt more dragged than eagerly moving forward, a paradigm shift was taking place. And the road we were on didn't have a fork ahead. It led straight into the glories of sovereign grace, and there was no turning back.

The Great God of Isaiah

My spiritual knees buckled under the sheer weight of God's glory in Isaiah. The chapters confronted, assaulted, and rebuked me: "Your view of God is too small!" His sovereignty permeated every chapter, sometimes in strong language that left me reeling. God commissioned Isaiah to preach to people whom he still intended to judge (Isa 6:10). He brought to pass what he planned and decreed (37:26). He upheld his glory and refused to share it with idols (42:8). He created people for his glory (43:7). No one could overturn his act of deliverance (43:13). He raised up political leaders who never trusted in him (45:5). He claimed that he would do anything that pleased him

(46:10). He is even referred to as sovereign (50:4-5, 7, 9). His word accomplished what he sent it to do (55:10-11). He was the potter who could harden hearts (63:17; 64:8).

Despite my struggle to understand God's sovereignty, the book of Isaiah portrayed a huge and daunting view of God. New theological convictions were forming, and no one was more surprised by it than me. When the semester on Isaiah ended, my understanding of God's word and ways had undergone significant changes. Though I initially felt pulled toward a certain view of sovereignty I had resisted up to that point, biblical texts convinced me of the conclusions found in the following chapters.

I even added new authors to my reading list. College friends had previously put in my hands books by John Piper and R. C. Sproul — I just never read them! But cracking their pages for the first time was like removing the cover off a deep well of insight and biblical fidelity. My list of names grew to include John MacArthur, J. I. Packer, D. A. Carson, Thomas Schreiner, and others. Since then, nothing has been the same, and I wouldn't have it any other way. Suffice it to say that I love the doctrine of God's total and meticulous sovereignty. In the last ten years, it has changed my life more than any other biblical teaching.

The Journey Ahead

Let's survey the landscape of what lies ahead. Chapters 1 and 5 form a frame around the middle three. Chapter 1 focuses on how God's sovereignty is manifested in creation, while chapter 5 looks at his control of history and the future. Chapters 2 through 4 highlight specific subjects frequently mentioned in conversations about this doctrine. Chapter 2 addresses sin and suffering, chapter 3 discusses the death of Jesus, and chapter 4 deals with salvation and judgment.

In this brief treatment of the doctrine, I want to demonstrate biblically that the scope of God's sovereignty is total, its reality for the believer should bring comfort, and its embrace should stir affections of worship. Our journey will not be easy and, at times, will be controversial. So here are three recommendations.

First, Read This Book with an Open Bible

In the end what matters is the Bible, not philosophical speculations. And a dominant theme of the Bible is certainly the sovereignty of God, so it would be unfortunate to neglect such a significant topic if our goal is to learn more of the Bible.[4] After all, God's sovereignty overlaps with so many other subjects (e.g. prayer, missions, worship, hope, salvation, suffering, judgment) that to neglect its study would prevent understanding them more fully.

---

4   Eugene Merrill has rightly observed, "…the notion of divine sovereignty that finds its roots in Genesis and other early texts remains a dominant one throughout the canonical testimony" (*Everlasting Dominion: A Theology of the Old Testament* [Nashville: B&H Publishing Group, 2006], 44).

Therefore, it would be wise to have a Bible nearby as you read this book. When I cite Scriptures in whole or in part, my aim is to honor the context of the verse(s), but independent confirmation with your own Bible will help assess whether my arguments are truly based in the text. If I am making claims that cannot be demonstrated from the Bible, then my conclusions should be suspended until such support can be found.

However, if you note that biblically-based arguments seem to be undermining your presuppositions about how God works in his world, I hope you'll commit yourself to follow the conclusions of the Bible — which may mean foregoing some initial assumptions. Our goal is to learn what the Bible teaches about the sovereignty of God, so it must be our ultimate authority and guide.

Second, Read This Book with an Open Mind

The question isn't whether or not you have a view of God's sovereignty. As a result of your culture, family, church, and life experiences, you have already drawn conclusions about this doctrine. The issue, then, is your view's *biblical cohesion*. Your prayer should be that the Lord, through his word, would correct any doctrinal deviations as well as confirm doctrinally sound assumptions.

I know it's a tall order, but I'm asking for your open-mindedness. First an open Bible, then an open mind. It's impossible to approach this book with a clean mental slate. What I have in view is the willingness to be self-critical, to question already-held presuppositions and previously-drawn conclusions.

Your willingness to be self-critical will help cultivate a humble reception of these chapters. I commend them as my best brief effort to engage the doctrine of God's sovereignty in relation to creation, sin, suffering, the death of Jesus, salvation, judgment, history, and the future.

Third, Read This Book Again With Someone

Go through the material once yourself. Afterward, discuss the content of the book with someone else. Constructive dialogue with other believers about God's sovereignty can be spiritually beneficial. Doctrines of the Christian faith should not be divorced from the community of faith. Seeking such dialogue might mean a second reading of some or all of the chapters with another person or a group of people. Open Bible, open mind, open dialogue.

Second trips through a book also provide a chance for processing and review. We don't always recall what we read once. Moreover, this particular doctrine is complex and multifaceted. Rereading the book can help you absorb the material. While I hope to convince you of my positions in the next five chapters, rereading them will at least reinforce comprehension of my arguments.

A Note about the Title

This book's title, *Behold Our Sovereign God*, summarizes what I hope will happen while you read and when you finish. I hope learning about God's sovereignty will leave you awestruck, astounded, amazed, and joyful. My prayer is that this doctrine would become a continual source of comfort and fuel for worship. I want you to behold him.

1

A Tapestry of Majesty: The Sovereignty of God over Creation

"Creation sings the Father's song;
He calls the sun to wake the dawn
And run the course of day,
Till evening falls with crimson rays.

His fingerprints in flakes of snow,
His breath upon this spinning globe.
He charts the eagle's flight,
Commands the newborn baby's cry."

From "Creation Sings the Father's Song"
by Keith and Kristyn Getty

This world is amazing, dare I say even *magical*. As we age and learn, sometimes we struggle to keep the same wonder toward the world we had as children, so it's helpful to see how children react to nature. When our son Jensen was two, he was afraid of leaves when a gust of wind tossed them around. The wind would blow, leaves would move, and he would hide behind my leg as I smiled. Leaves just seemed to rise up from the ground and dance in the air for no reason at all.

Here in Louisville the leaves recently changed color and fell to the ground. At parks Jensen, now three, loves to find one the size of his head and carry it around. He's fascinated by nature. Tomorrow is the first day of winter, and snow and ice already cover the grass and roads. He's been around such weather before, but he's never noticed it like this.

It's good to see wonder in the eyes of a child because the enchantment of God's world can become normal, even mundane. How tragic! This is my Father's world, and it is majestic.

Total Control in Undisturbed Majesty

Deism is the belief that God created the world but is not personally interacting with it. He simply jumpstarted the project and lets it run its course. The goings-on of nature are nothing more than the inevitable results of microscopic systems at work.

But deism is incompatible with passages like Colossians 1:16-17, "For by him all things were created, in heaven and on earth, visible and invisible, whether thrones or dominions or rulers or authorities — all things were created through him and for him. And he is before all things, and in him all things hold together."

Michael Lewis sees the implication of Paul's words: "The creation is neither self-existent nor self-sustaining; because of this, God, by a continuous and direct agency must preserve the creation, that is, maintain in existence what he has created."[5]

God is running his world. He is in charge, and he is what keeps it going.

The Bible teaches the comprehensive sovereignty of God, from the edges of space to the baby in a womb. One way of showing this would be to present what each book of the Bible contributes to the doctrine of divine sovereignty, but that approach is beyond the scope of this work. Instead I have chosen five categories of creation and will reflect on Bible passages pertaining to them. We will look at God's sovereignty over the heavens, the earth, the weather, animals, and people.

At the end of this chapter I hope you will see the truth of Loraine Boettner's words about God: "He exerts not merely a general influence, but actually rules in the world which He has created....Amid all the apparent defeats and inconsistencies of life God actually moves on in undisturbed majesty."[6]

---

5   Michael E. Lewis, *A Theology of Suffering and Difficulty: Corporate and Personal Aspects* (Eugene: Wipf & Stock, 2006), 24.

6   Loraine Boettner, *The Reformed Doctrine of Predestination* (Phillipsburg: Presbyterian and Reformed Publishing Company, 1932), 30.

The Heavens

While I cannot process the vastness of the universe, my ears are receiving an important message: *Behold the glory of God!* "The heavens declare the glory of God, and the sky above proclaims his handiwork....Their voice goes out through all the earth, and their words to the end of the world" (Ps 19:1, 4).

When we look into space, we are seeing the majesty of God. "God created the universe not as an object of academic scrutiny but as an arena in which he can display something of his nature and intentions."[7] And when we behold his revelation, it should lead to our adoration. If your telescope isn't an instrument of worship, you're not using it correctly.

High-powered telescopes have revealed how immense the universe is, bigger than our minds can comprehend. But if life is never found elsewhere in the universe, God has not wasted any space — literally. Every galaxy exists for the glory of God. The purpose of every planet and star is to proclaim the greatness of the God who made them.

The full expanse of the heavens is like a curtain God stretches out or like a tent he spreads to dwell in (Isa 40:22). Solomon asked, "Who is able to build him a house, since heaven, even highest heaven, cannot contain him?" (2 Chron 2:6a). While God's creation is indeed great, God is greater. While the heavens are glorious, their glory is a

---

7   Eugene Merrill, *Everlasting Dominion: A Theology of the Old Testament* (Nashville: B&H Publishing Group, 2006), 129-30.

stage for his majesty. "The glory of creation and the glory of God are as different as the love poem and the love, the painting and the landscape, the ring and the marriage."[8]

God's eternal power and divine nature are evident in what he has made, so sinners have no excuse for turning their backs on him (Rom 1:20). Orbiting planets, falling stars, shooting asteroids, complex constellations — the heavens are full of outrageous beauty, but their beauty is derivative. There is no self-made majesty in the heavens.

The opening words of Scripture teach that before creation there was only God, and everything he made came into being because he commanded they show up. Have you ever thought about God's power exercised in the words, "Let there be light" (Gen 1:3)? N. D. Wilson is right: "You are spoken. I am spoken. We stand on a spoken stage. The spinning kind. The round kind. The moist kind."[9] Earth, moon, stars — God made them all using nothing but sovereign syllables (Gen 1:16-18). "By the word of the LORD the heavens were made, and by the breath of his mouth all their host" (Ps 33:6).

God created the heavenly entities for his own glory and as a display of his greatness, and he wants us to know it. "Lift up your eyes on high and see: who created these? He who brings out their host by number, calling them all by name, by the greatness of his might, and because he

---

8   John Piper, *The Pleasures of God: Meditations on God's Delight in Being God* (Sisters: Multnomah, 2000), 85.

9   N. D. Wilson, *Notes from the Tilt-A-Whirl: Wide-Eyed Wonder in God's Spoken World* (Nashville: Thomas Nelson, 2009), 24.

is strong in power not one is missing" (Isa 40:26; cf. Ps 147:4). Think of it: God never loses something he's made and then has to search for it. Rather, he brings out the heavenly host according to their exact number. Every star is where it should be each night, displaying the glory of its Maker.

Agreeing with Paul's words to the Colossians, the writer of Hebrews said Jesus "upholds the universe by the word of his power" (1:3a). He doesn't sustain only some things or most things but *the whole universe*. Modern science describes how the natural world functions, but it also marginalizes or ignores the comprehensive sovereignty of Jesus. This is tragic, since he should be praised as Lord over everything.[10]

The Earth

The topic of the universe is broad, so let's move to the earth. Like the heavens, the third rock from the sun is a masterpiece of God's handiwork. Wet water, warm sunrays, crunchy leaves, rough bark, soft petals, prickly thorns, firm ground — these realities warrant our recognition but often go unnoticed.

---

10 A coordinate truth to the teaching that Jesus sustains the universe is his preeminence over all things. Jesus existed before everything (Jn 1:2-3; Col 1:17a), all things were made by him and through him (1 Cor 8:6; Col 1:16; Heb 1:2), all things exist for him (Col 1:16), and he is the heir of all things (Col 1:15; Heb 1:2). The Son of God is supremely sovereign.

Believers throughout the Scripture were not deists. They believed God was involved with what he made on this spinning globe. David asserted, "The earth is the LORD's and the fullness thereof" (Ps 24:1). When God made the earth he declared his creation good (Gen 1:3-31). He alone laid the foundation of the earth and determined its measurements (Job 38:4-5). He still sets the boundaries for the sea and says to the waves, "Thus far shall you come, and no farther" (Job 38:8, 11).

Morning always arrives at his command (Job 38:12), and he makes the sun rise on the righteous and the unrighteous (Matt 5:45). None of us deserves the gift of a new day's dawn, but God has given millions of them. Another one showed up this morning.

On the land, God makes grass grow on hills (Ps 147:8) and fields (Matt 6:30). He can turn rivers into a desert (Ps 107:33-34) as well as a desert into springs of water (107:35). The mountains and valleys are where God appointed them (104:8), and their heights and depths are in his hands (95:4). He plants trees for the birds to nest (104:16-17). He causes plants to grow and brings forth food from the earth (104:14). Bounty and abundance come from him (65:11). And he does these things without consulting any of us! He is God all by himself.

These truths amaze me, but I'm certain we are not as awestruck by God ruling and sustaining the earth as we should be. The texts in the preceding paragraphs may challenge our assumptions about how God works in the world. *Could he really be this involved with the details of creation? Should I really think of God making grass grow? Shouldn't I thank him for creating the sun but still expect it to rise apart from his control?*

We need the Bible to inform and conform our view of the world. God is Creator and Provider, Lord and Sustainer. Not only should we embrace the Bible's teaching about God's rule over creation, we should exalt him for it! The book of Psalms was the songbook for the people of God. They saw his good hand behind what took place in the world, and they wanted to *sing* about his sovereignty. His sovereignty should stir our praise, not stifle it.

Weather

If God controls the details of the heavens and the earth, he is in control of weather. The psalmist said, "Praise the LORD from the earth, you great sea creatures and all deeps, fire and hail, snow and mist, stormy wind *fulfilling his word!*" (Ps 148:7-8). Elihu told Job, "For to the snow he says, 'Fall on the earth,' likewise to the downpour, his mighty downpour" (Job 37:6). Also, "From its chamber comes the whirlwind, and cold from the scattering winds. By the breath of God ice is given, and the broad waters are frozen fast" (37:9-10).

God asked Job, "Have you entered the storehouses of the snow, or have you seen the storehouses of the hail, which I have reserved for the time of trouble, for the day of battle and war?" (Job 38:22-23). No, Job hadn't.

"Can you lift up your voice to the clouds, that a flood of waters may cover you? Can you send forth lightnings, that they may go and say to you, 'Here we are'?" (Job 38:34-35). No, Job couldn't.

Elihu said, "[God] loads the thick cloud with moisture; the clouds scatter his lightning. They turn around and around by his guidance, to accomplish all that he commands them on the face of the habitable world" (Job 37:11-12).

When you witness manifestations of weather, where do you think they originate? "For the Hebrews, rain did not simply happen; God sent the rain. They saw him as the all-powerful determiner of everything that occurs. Not only is he active in everything that occurs, but he has planned it."[11] Lightning, hail, snow, rain, and wind all obey his command.

And God commands the weather apart from external constraints. "Whatever the LORD pleases, he does, in heaven and on earth, in the seas and all deeps" (Ps 135:6). He acts according to his *pleasure*. The fallen world's weather has not somehow wrested itself from God's grasp. "He sends out his command to the earth; his word runs swiftly. He gives snow like wool; he scatters hoarfrost like ashes. He hurls down his crystals of ice like crumbs....He sends out his word, and melts them; he makes his wind blow and the waters flow" (Ps 147:15-18). Reflecting on Psalm

---

11   Millard J. Erickson, *Christian Theology*, 2nd ed. (Grand Rapids: Baker Books, 1998), 374.

147, John Frame wrote, "Notice the monergism in these statements: these are things that God does, because they please him. He does not merely allow them to happen; rather, *he makes them happen*" (emphasis mine).[12]

Do storms make you think about the power of God? When you see snow or rain, you are beholding the fulfillment of God's word. When you feel wind blow or watch lightning split the sky, you are watching obedience in action. Sometimes rain is gentle and refreshes the land, while other times it becomes a torrential flood. Snow may create beautiful scenery, but the fury of a blizzard can cause widespread damage and injury.

No matter the type or effects of weather in this world, the Bible consistently affirms the sovereignty of God over it all. Meteorologists project what the days ahead will look like, but their predictions ultimately give way to God's sovereign decree. God doesn't forecast, he foreordains.

Animals

When first confronted with the doctrine of divine sovereignty, I didn't reflect much on God's rule over animals, but the Bible is filled with examples of it. The very existence of animals displays God's wisdom: "O LORD, how manifold are your works! In wisdom have you made them all; the earth is full of your creatures" (Ps 104:24).

---

12   John M. Frame, *The Doctrine of God* (Phillipsburg: P&R, 2002), 51.

After God made the sea creatures and the birds, he told them to multiply and fill the waters and skies (Gen 1:20-22). Then he made land creatures and saw that they were good (1:24-25). Not only does the Lord create them, he cares for them and sustains them by providing food (1:30) and other things they need to survive. He feeds the birds (Job 38:41; Ps 147:9; Matt 6:26a) and the beasts (Ps 147:9). God clothes the horse's neck with a mane (Job 39:19), he gives water to animals in the field (Ps 104:10-11), causes grass to grow for livestock (104:14), plants trees for birds (104:16-17), and forms high mountains for wild goats (104:18). Animals are dependent on divine provision.

God rules over the life of animals. Eagles make nests at his command to prepare their eggs for hatching (Job 39:27), and his voice makes deer give birth (Ps 29:9a). God also rules over the death of his creatures. A sparrow doesn't fall to the ground apart from his will (Matt 10:29). Once, he even destroyed "every living thing that was on the face of the ground" (Gen 7:23a).

Sometimes animals were instruments of divine judgment. In Exodus, God summoned different ones for some of the plagues upon Egypt (Ex 7 – 12). "[God] turned their waters into blood and caused their fish to die. Their land swarmed with frogs, even in the chambers of their kings. He spoke, and there came swarms of flies, and gnats throughout their country....He spoke, and the locusts came, young locusts without number" (Ps 105:29-31, 34).

There are biblical narratives in addition to those found in Genesis and Exodus that portray God's sovereignty over animals. While Balaam rode on a donkey, God opened its mouth and caused it to speak (Num 22:28)! In 1 Kings 17, Elijah received this word from the Lord, "Depart from here and turn eastward and hide yourself by the brook Cherith, which is east of the Jordan. You shall drink from the brook, and *I have commanded the ravens* to feed you there" (17:3-4).

The story of Jonah also demonstrates God's supreme rule over creatures. After the prophet's shipmates threw him overboard, the Lord "appointed a great fish to swallow up Jonah" (Jon 1:17a). Three days and three nights later, God "spoke to the fish, and it vomited Jonah out upon the dry land" (2:10). When the Lord was meeting with Jonah at a later date, he appointed a worm to attack a plant (4:7).

The story of Daniel in the lions' den is an example of God sovereignly using the same animals for different purposes. When Daniel broke his Persian king's injunction not to pray to the Lord, King Darius commanded that he be cast into the den of lions (Dan 6:7-8, 12-13, 17). The next day Darius went to the den and discovered Daniel was still alive. The man of God relayed what happened: "My God sent his angel and shut the lions' mouths, and they have not harmed me" (Dan 6:22a).

Then Darius ordered that those who had accused Daniel be thrown into the den of lions. "And before they reached the bottom of the den, the lions overpowered them and broke all their bones in pieces" (Dan 6:24b). So the Lord was sovereign over the deliverance of Daniel and the deaths of Daniel's accusers.

God reigns supreme over animals. He made them, sustains them, and uses them for his purposes. They cannot act against what he has decreed. Since animals are part of God's creation, we should praise him for their existence. Animals can be fun, comforting, and helpful. They can be loyal companions, and they can be food. But they should never be objects of worship. Sinful man has often "exchanged the glory of the immortal God for images resembling...birds and animals and creeping things" (Rom 1:23). The sovereign creator, not representations of his creation, should be worshiped.

People

Have you ever considered the details of your life in view of God's sovereignty? Do you believe events in your life are random or meaningless? Are you the captain of your soul, the master of your fate? In this subsection, we will focus on God's sovereignty over the non-spiritual elements of our lives.[13] I've dedicated chapter 4 to the discussion of God's sovereignty over salvation and judgment. So while spiritual questions may be prompted by this section, I will postpone them for now.

Consider the years your life has spanned so far. When my wife Stacie watches movies set in past centuries, she often comments on the elaborate dresses of the ladies. "I

---

13   I'm referring here to the elements which are not essentially salvific.

wish I lived back then so I could wear that. It's so beautiful, so elegant!"

But *when* you live is no accident. Paul told the Athenians, "[God] made from one man every nation of mankind to live on all the face of the earth, having determined allotted periods and the boundaries of their dwelling place" (Acts 17:26). In other words, God sovereignly determines when and where cultures develop. You had no control over when or where you were born.

The Bible also affirms God's sovereignty over our conception and development. He opens (Gen 25:21; 29:31) and closes wombs (Gen 20:18; 1 Sam 1:5) and even guides development *inside* the womb: "For you formed my inward parts; you knitted me together in my mother's womb. I praise you, for I am fearfully and wonderfully made....My frame was not hidden from you, when I was being made in secret, intricately woven in the depths of the earth" (Ps 139:13-15).

Sometimes during or after development a person faces various physical challenges, but this doesn't happen because God has lost control. God is sovereign over any physical (in)ability. When Moses cited slowness of speech as a reason why he should not speak to the Israelites about the judgment coming on Egypt, God said to him, "Who has made man's mouth? Who makes him mute, or deaf, or seeing, or blind? Is it not I, the LORD?" (Ex 4:11).

The presence of a handicap doesn't handicap God, for the New Testament shows he has the power to correct it, whether the person was born with it or incurred it later.

Jesus healed an invalid (John 5:8-9), granted sight to a blind man (9:6-7), enabled a mute man to speak (Matt 9:33), restored a leper's withered hand (12:13), and raised a dead man four days after the heart stopped beating (John 11:44).

We should be in awe at God's sovereignty over the details of life. Once, when he was encouraging his disciples to persevere despite the temptation to deny him before persecutors, Jesus assured them of the heavenly Father's care. "Even the hairs of your head are all numbered" (Matt 10:30). And the color of those hairs is under the sway of God's will too (5:36).

In addition to numbering our hairs, God has numbered our *days*. He wrote them before one ever came to be: "… in your book were written, every one of them, the days that were formed for me" (Ps 139:16). He determined the months and years of a man (Job 14:5), and this limit cannot be known or trespassed. "[I]f He has the authority to choose my parents, my race, my birthplace, my height, my intelligence, the size of my tonsils; if He has the authority to design my teeth from scratch, then He has the authority to choose my end."[14]

This secret determination shouldn't paralyze our lives. It is not wrong to make plans, but we must remember that they hinge on God's will. Those who boast about their plans should instead say, "If the Lord wills, we will live and do this or that" (Jam 4:15). God is sovereign over our itinerary.

---

14   Wilson, *Notes from the Tilt-A-Whirl*, 112.

Not just our doing but our *living* is contingent on his will. He "gives to all mankind life and breath and everything" (Acts 17:25). The involuntary exercise of inhaling and exhaling is in his hands (Job 12:10) because he holds our breath (Dan 5:23).

All these truths about God's sovereignty have an inescapable implication: we have never experienced anything random. Nothing just happens. In God's world, he exerts control over the details, and no detail is too insignificant. Consider the casting of lots: "The lot is cast into the lap, but its every decision is from the LORD" (Prov 16:33). The wise writer has given us an instance that seems, from a human perspective, left to chance. But readers of the Bible know better. Not even a cast lot is outside his decree.

The Bible shows God's sovereignty over happenstance in narratives like the one about King Ahab and the aimless archer. God had decreed destruction against King Ahab, but the king thought he could escape it. He disguised himself and went into battle to blend in and avoid being sought, identified, and killed. But "a certain man drew his bow *at random* and struck the king of Israel between the scale armor and the breastplate" (1 Kgs 22:34a).

God guided the flight of a "random" arrow to hit the exact person (Ahab) in precisely the right place (between the armor and breastplate). The archer did not plan to hit Ahab, but God did. And God never misses.

From the first breath to the last, our lives are in the hands of a sovereign God.

Conclusion

At this point you may have questions, even objections, to the conclusions presented in this chapter. *So is everything already determined? If God is in total control of the universe, doesn't that make us puppets of a divine puppeteer? Does this mean God has ultimately decreed all things that ever happen?*

We'll start seeing some of the answers in the next chapter. For now I submit the preceding Scriptural passages as partial evidence of what it means for God to be sovereign.[15] While it may seem strange to us, the biblical writers unashamedly attributed to their reigning Creator the operation of the heavens, the earth, the weather, the animals, and their own lives.

"All things, both in heaven and earth, from the seraphim down to the tiny atom, are ordered by His never-failing providence."[16]

---

15 Merrill says, "Any view of God that assigns him any role other than that of sovereign over all creation results either in an ontological dualism in which he is coequal with the material and/or spiritual universe or at least renders him limited in some aspects of his nature and work" (*Everlasting Dominion*, 646).

16 Boettner, *The Reformed Doctrine of Predestination*, 35.

2

From the Mouth of the Most High: The Sovereignty of God over Sin and Suffering

"Judge not the Lord by feeble sense,
But trust him for his grace;
Behind a frowning providence
He hides a smiling face.

Blind unbelief is sure to err,
And scan his work in vain.
God is his own interpreter,
And he will make it plain."

From "God Moves in a Mysterious Way" by William Cowper

A few months ago I watched an interview with a man whose family had been murdered. He held back tears as he recounted his pain, grief, and depression. The conversation turned to faith, a subject which had not brought him much comfort. With brutal transparency he said, "I think that some things in the world are simply out of God's control."

Many people agree with the man's assertion, especially those who have gone through similar or worse experiences. But the question is, while it may appear that some things are out of God's control, is that actually the case?

What the Bible Says about God and Evil

People across the millennia have endured varying degrees of suffering, and a common question has united many of them: if a good and powerful God exists, why is there so much sin and suffering in the world?

Evangelical Christians affirm that God could at any moment, if he wanted, eliminate all suffering. This leads to the next affirmation: if God can end evil yet doesn't, then he must have some purpose for it. This is where things get shaky, as we may not see how evil serves a purpose in God's plan. Instead, evil seems to oppose God's plan, to seek to subvert it at every turn.

We need the Bible to give feeble feet a firm place to stand. Even as we start this difficult topic, I hope you'll agree with Bruce Ware:

> The sole criterion for understanding the nature of divine sovereignty is simply this: whatever God tells us in Scripture about his lordship and sovereign rulership over the universe is what we should believe, because this alone can be the infallible truth about his sovereignty....From the beginning of the Bible

to the end (quite literally), readers are constantly encouraged, in account after account, to think of God as in control of what takes place in this world.[17]

And since the Bible is not silent on the matter, we should know and believe what it says about the extent of God's lordship in his world. Sometimes in dealing with a subject we must settle for mystery though we desire greater clarity, but not everything is unknown. Even mysteries may still have true things said about them. So may we avoid the grave but common error of being frustrated with what is unclear and consequently denying what *is* clear.

One caveat before we proceed. Sometimes in the task of theology we attempt to understand what is beyond our reach, so we should prepare ourselves to not have all our questions answered. Our comprehension capacity is limited, and our reason is affected by sin. These two realities make reliance on divine revelation that much more important, for apart from Christ our thinking is futile (Rom 1:21). We claimed to be wise but were fools (Rom 1:22), exchanging God's truth for lies (Rom 1:25). God gave us over to a debased mind (Rom 1:28), and we deserved nothing less.

Therefore, as we think and reason, we must do so in submission to Scripture. Our thinking may sometimes steer us wrong, but Scripture will always steer us right.

---

17 Bruce A. Ware, *God's Greater Glory: The Exalted God of Scripture and the Christian Faith* (Wheaton: Crossway Books, 2004), 67.

Evil's Beginning is Unexplained

Something happened prior to Genesis 3 which isn't narrated. As far as the reader of the narrative knows, an evil tempter suddenly enters God's good paradise to seduce and deceive. He goes after the woman first with a string of seedy remarks, questioning God's word (Gen 3:1), stimulating suspicion of God's warning not to eat from a certain tree (Gen 3:4), and implying shady motives behind God's command (Gen 3:5). Even before Eve and Adam taste the forbidden fruit, the reader recognizes something has already gone wrong.

Though evil entered paradise through the seducing serpent, its origin is unexplained. How did Satan rebel against his Maker? If God originally created all things good — angels included — then how was Satan tempted, especially if there was neither a tempter nor any internal and twisted inclinations that would lead him astray? We simply don't know. Genesis 3 narrates man's fall, not Satan's.

In his book *Evil and the Justice of God*, N. T. Wright describes our concerns:

> We want to know what evil really is, why it's there in the first place (or at least in the second place), why it's been allowed to continue, and how long this will go on. These questions are in the Bible, but frustratingly they don't receive very full answers, and certainly not the sort of answers that later philosophical traditions would consider adequate.[18]

18   N. T. Wright, *Evil and the Justice of God* (Downers Grove: IVP Books, 2006), 44.

To compound the matter, the existence of evil is a problem for Christians in a unique way. In contrast to other worldviews,

> ...we Christians believe that there is one living God, the creator of the whole universe, who is personal, good, loving, omnipotent, and sovereign over all that happens. Now once you are convinced of those great biblical truths about the living God, you cannot help but have a massive problem with the existence of evil....Unquestionably, the Bible affirms that God is all-loving and all-powerful, and yet the Bible also describes the terrible reality of evil.[19]

Although the origin of evil is not specified in the Bible, the pages of Scripture are filled with examples of wickedness and suffering. These manifestations can be categorized as *natural evil* (disasters such as hurricanes, tsunamis, fires) and *moral evil* (human sins). In this chapter I will address both categories, as well as the suffering they frequently cause.

God Decrees Sin and Suffering

My claim is twofold: God ordains sin and suffering, and he is not evil in doing so. This subsection will defend the first part of my claim, and the next subsection will

---

19   Christopher J. H. Wright, *The God I Don't Understand: Reflections on Tough Questions of Faith* (Grand Rapids: Zondervan, 2008), 27.

address the second part. Biblically-speaking, both parts stand or fall together.

The LORD gives and takes away. If we're going to talk about suffering and God's will, Job is a perfect place to start. Job is an example of a man who learned hard theological lessons during trials. Theology tested in the furnace of affliction is petrifying and purifying.

All in one day he lost his oxen and donkeys (Job 1:14-15), sheep (1:16), camels (1:17), servants (1:15, 16, 17), and children (1:18). And the most important outcome of that day's tragedy was his interpretation of the events: "Naked I came from my mother's womb, and naked shall I return. The LORD gave, and the LORD has taken away; blessed be the name of the LORD" (Job 1:21).

Job did not believe his children and servants perished because God lost control. He believed God took them. Maybe your instinct is to say, *Job was simply theologically misguided by attributing the tragedy to God.* That very idea appeared in a recent magazine article written by a Christian dealing with loss. To him Job 1:21 represented unenlightened thoughts which would be refined and corrected as the book progressed. At the time, though, Job's words were untrue — more than that, they were bad theology! Attributing the tragedy to God's hand was unthinkable. Job simply didn't know any better yet, but soon he would.

Saying Job 1:21 is "bad theology" may sound like an appealing position to some interpreters, but the very next verse flatly rejects it. The narrator says, "In all this Job did not sin or charge God with wrong" (Job 1:22). We mustn't pass quickly by these words. The phrase "In all this" refers to the words just spoken. If God didn't take Job's children and servants yet Job claimed he did, Job would be making a false charge—which would be sinful to do.

The narrator steers the reader right into the doctrine of divine sovereignty. Job wasn't incorrect to say, "The LORD gave, and the LORD has taken away." But a further thing must be observed. Is it possible that Job *correctly* spoke about something God had *wrongly* done? After all, it's possible for us to accurately recount the wrong committed by someone.

But the narrator assures us, "Job did not...charge God with wrong." Job was right in what he said, and God was right in what he did.

God is sovereign over secondary causes. The situation is a bit more complicated than just saying, "God took Job's children, servants, and livestock." While the words of Job 1:21 are certainly true, other factors come into play as well: Satan (1:6-12), the Sabeans (1:15), fire (1:16), the Chaldeans (1:17), and a great wind (1:19).

These factors are all *secondary* causes, and the text narrates their respective roles in the story:

- God had previously said to Satan, "Behold, all that [Job] has is in your hand" (1:12a).
- The Sabeans took Job's oxen and donkeys and killed his servants (1:15).
- A fire from heaven burned the sheep and consumed more servants (1:16).

- The Chaldeans took his camels and killed even more of his servants (1:17).
- A great wind caused his oldest son's house to fall fatally upon the other siblings (1:19).

But Job didn't attribute his loss to any of these secondary factors, for he knew something we must learn from the Bible: *God is sovereign over secondary causes.* Yes, Satan opposed, the Sabeans attacked, the fire fell, the Chaldeans raided, and the wind blew, but it is not wrong to say that *God* took away.

The secondary causes (which included a natural disaster like catastrophic wind as well as moral evils like thievery and murder) were not outside of God's control. *God* was the one who prompted Satan's interest by suggesting Job (1:8), and then he limited the degree of Satan's opposition by saying, "Behold, all that he has is in your hand. Only against him do not stretch out your hand" (Job 1:12). Job might have been in Satan's hand, but both Job and Satan were in God's.

At the end of the book, Job confessed to God, "I know that you can do all things, and no purpose of yours can be thwarted" (42:2). Secondary causes serve, not thwart, the mysterious purposes of our wise and sovereign God.

God sends both good and evil. As if the first chapter of Job isn't enough to provoke numerous questions and deep anxiety, the second chapter ups the ante. God *again* suggests his servant Job to Satan (2:3) and *again* limits the degree of Satan's opposition against the man—Satan is now able to afflict Job directly but not fatally (2:6). "So Satan went out from the presence of the LORD and struck Job with loathsome soars from the sole of his foot to the crown of his head" (2:7).

Though Job lost his livestock, servants, children, and even his health, he still maintains his integrity (Job 2:3, 9a). His wife, on the other hand, considers Job's perseverance foolish. She thinks she's married to an idiot who will just take whatever comes his way. "Curse God and die!" she said (2:9b). Job and his wife contrast one another in their responses to suffering, and their responses are typical of how we see people behave: some maintain their integrity before God, others think cursing God is a better alternative.

But before Job's wife demanded he turn against God, she used a phrase we've seen already. Satan had heard God say that Job "still holds fast his integrity," and now Job's wife complains with the *same phrase*, "Do you still hold fast your integrity?" (2:9a). With words pleasing to the Tempter's ears she tempts Job to blaspheme God.

If your spouse told you to shake your fist at God and then drop dead, what would your next words be? Job responds with a rebuke: "You speak as one of the foolish women would speak" (2:10a). She might think she married a fool, but Job knows the sound of ridiculous advice when he hears it. She is the true fool here. Her words are satanic.

Then Job asks her a question. "Shall we receive good from God, and shall we not receive evil?" (2:10b). Her bad wisdom encounters a massive theological proposition, and it smashes her foolishness flat. It isn't surprising that good would come from God. Who would deny that? But *evil*? That's another issue entirely. And the phrasing "Shall we... and shall we not" suggests that Job not only thought he received evil from God, he said it should be expected.

Perhaps you're thinking, *I object to Job's conclusion. Evil coming from God? It's not only wrong, it's blasphemy!*

Not so fast. He who has ears let him hear the narrator's assurance: "In all this Job *did not sin* with his lips" (Job 2:10c). The text doesn't say, "In all this Job blasphemed with his lips" or "In all this Job spoke foolishly of receiving evil from God." The narrator saw our objection coming before we ever made it.

The Bible gives us verbs. Part of the struggle in a discussion like this is choosing how to speak about God's relationship to sin and suffering. Commonly used words include *permit* and *allow*, which certainly aren't wrong. After all, didn't God permit Satan to afflict Job? Didn't God allow Job's children to be killed by a collapsing house and his servants to be struck down by advancing armies?

Narratives like Job 1−2 imply God's allowance and permission. The tension is in balancing this with the other words, words used by the key character and endorsed by the narrator. I am concerned that we may only use words like *permit* or *allow* because we fear ones which make us uncomfortable. John Frame believes it is appropriate to use the term *permission*, but "we should not assume...

that divine permission is anything less than sovereign ordination."[20]

We should become increasingly comfortable using the Bible's verbs to describe the Bible's God.

God intends or prevents evil for a reason. In thinking about how to speak of God's relationship to sin and suffering, we need to incorporate more biblical texts, and the last chapter of Genesis contributes a valuable piece to this puzzle. Joseph's brothers feared he would avenge himself for the evil they committed against him (Gen 50:15), but he told them, "As for you, you meant evil against me, but God meant it for good" (Gen 50:20).

Joseph's interpretation of his experiences is important, because he said that God *intended* them to happen. God intended the sins and suffering of Joseph's betrayal by his brothers, his near death, his enslavement, and his Egyptian imprisonment to occur. The difference between his brothers and God was not that they intended Joseph's suffering while God did not. The difference was in the respective

---

20   John M. Frame, "The Problem of Evil," in *Suffering and the Goodness of God*, Theology in Community, ed. Christopher W. Morgan and Robert A. Peterson (Wheaton: Crossway Books, 2008), 161. He also writes, "Therefore, there has been much discussion among theologians as to what verb best describes God's agency in regard to evil. Some initial possibilities: *authors, brings out, causes, controls, creates, decrees, foreordains, incites, includes within his plan, makes happen, ordains, permits, plans, predestines, predetermines, produces, stands behind,* and *wills*....So theologians need to consider carefully which of these terms, if any, should be affirmed, and in what sense. Words are the theologian's tools. In a situation like this, none of the possibilities is fully adequate. Each term has its advantages and disadvantages" (157-58).

designs of the suffering—the brothers' intentions were evil, but God's were good.

The Bible illustrates God's sovereignty over sin in another story. In Genesis 20, Abraham journeyed to Gerar and hid the truth that Sarah was his wife. After King Abimelech took her (20:2), God came to him in a dream and threatened judgment because Sarah was married (20:3). When the king insisted on his integrity and innocence (20:5), God told him, "Yes, I know that you have done this in the integrity of your heart, and *it was I who kept you from sinning* against me. Therefore *I did not let you* touch her" (20:6). Consider what these words mean: God is sovereign over sin and can restrain or prevent it whenever he wants. Divine will trumps human will.

Just to be clear, God is not obligated to restrain sin prior to the final judgment, the appointed time when he will righteously punish evil. He is no less sovereign when sinners face consequences now for their sins. "He did not protect Adam and Eve from the Serpent, nor Abel from Cain, nor the daughters of men from tyrants, nor the earth from violence."[21]

To take this topic in another direction, one way God reveals his wrath against sin is by giving sinners over to their corrupt inclinations. Paul explains that God relinquishes sinners over to the lusts of their hearts (Rom 1:24), dishonorable passions (1:26), and a debased mind for

---

21   Bruce K. Waltke, *An Old Testament Theology: An Exegetical, Canonical, and Thematic Approach* (Grand Rapids: Zondervan, 2007), 286.

acts of disobedience (1:28). In such instances, God does not restrain the wicked from sinning but delivers them over for that very purpose.

Blessing and calamity come from God's mouth. God is sovereign over disaster, which multiple biblical texts confirm. The Preacher said, "In the day of prosperity be joyful, and in the day of adversity consider: God has made the one as well as the other" (Eccl 7:14). Through the prophet Amos, the Lord said, "Does disaster come to a city, unless the LORD has done it?" (Amos 3:6b). After the destruction of Jerusalem and the exile of God's people, a writer reflected, "Who has spoken and it came to pass, unless the Lord has commanded it? Is it not from the mouth of the Most High that good and bad come?" (Lam 3:37-38). Isaiah recorded God's claim, "I form light and create darkness, I make well-being and create calamity, I am the LORD, who does all these things" (Isa 45:7). In this string of verses, God causes, decrees, and creates disaster.

Space prevents adequate treatment of many other Scriptures which relate God's sovereignty to sin and suffering. God can harden hearts to ensure disobedience (Ex 4:21; Deut 2:30), raise up evil adversaries (Ex 9:16; 2 Sam 12:11; 1 Kgs 11:14, 23; Isa 44:28), send evil or harmful spirits (Judg 9:23; 1 Sam 16:14-16; 19:9; 1 Kgs 22:23; 2 Kgs 19:7; 2 Chron 18:22), cause evil to return onto an evildoer (1 Sam 25:39; Prov 16:4), ensure that harm comes to someone (2 Sam 17:14), send pestilence (2 Sam 24:15; 1 Chron 21:14), bring disaster (Ruth 1:20; 1 Kgs 9:9; Job 1:22; 2:10; Isa 45:7; Amos 3:6b), call for a famine (2 Kgs 8:1), use pagan nations to judge his people (2 Kgs 24:2; 2 Chron 21:16; Isa 45:1), and cause distress to a nation (2 Chron 15:6).

Sometimes the Bible describes God as directly sending evil or indirectly overseeing sin and suffering through secondary causes, but, either way, he is in control. Therefore, we shouldn't hesitate to use the Bible's language when talking about these matters. The words *allow* and *permit*, while appropriate to use, do not depict the full picture of God's sovereignty. We must incorporate biblical words such as *ordain*, *decree*, *create*, and *send* into our vocabulary.

The Hebrews saw the hand of God behind the events of the world. From his hand we receive both good and evil. From the mouth of the Most High come both blessing and calamity. God is sovereign over sin, suffering, and Satan.

God is Not Evil

So who is to blame for evil in the world? Given the previous section, it may seem logical to conclude that God, if he decrees evil, is culpable for it and is indeed evil himself. After all, sinners who plan iniquity are acting from their depravity, so why wouldn't God's decrees of evil proceed from divine depravity? This serious objection must not be ignored, for the character of God is at stake.

Biblical testimony creates a tension. While the cross will be specifically treated in the next chapter, Mark Talbot's words illustrate the difficulty of our current objection: "How can Pilate and Herod and Judas and the Jewish people be properly blamed for what God had predestined to take place?"[22] Shouldn't God be accountable for their wickedness?

These are tough questions, but there are answers. We will see from the Bible that man, not God, is guilty for wickedness in the world—we will answer to him, not he to us. And man, not God, is wicked—he is righteous and pure, not us.

So what should we do if our fallen minds insist that God cannot ordain evil without being evil? The short answer is this: remind ourselves that our reasoning doesn't always line up with the logic of God's inspired Bible. If we see the Bible's teaching and then make implications it clearly forbids, we should let it correct us. Our deductions aren't inspired, but God's are.

The Bible speaks of God sending evil yet being without sin himself, and such testimony forms a tension: how can they both be true? But this tension is an example of God's thoughts and ways being higher than ours (Isa 55:8). We should accept that it *is* this way without fully understanding *how*. Welcome to the realm of mystery.

---

22   Mark R. Talbot, "All the Good That Is Ours in Christ," in *Suffering and the Sovereignty of God*, ed. John Piper and Justin Taylor (Wheaton: Crossway Books, 2006), 69. He also wrote, "...our attempts to understand this involve our trying to understand the unique relationship between the Creator and his creatures in terms of our understanding of some creature-to-creature relationship. But these attempts, it should be obvious, involve us in a kind of 'category mistake' that dooms our attempts from the start. A 'category mistake' involves attempting to think about something under the wrong category. How the Creator's agency relates to his creatures' agency is to be categorized quite differently from how any creature's agency relates to any other creature's agency."

Acknowledgments of mystery aren't necessarily copouts, since we should expect conundrums from time to time. This is one of those times.

God is holy and hates sin. The Bible will not allow us to speak derisively about God's character, for it consistently asserts his purity and righteousness. He is merciful, gracious, patient, faithful, and loving (Exod 34:6). He hates pride, deception, murder, premeditated iniquity, reckless living, false testimony, and divisive people (Prov 6:17-19). Put succinctly, *God hates sin.*

But, according to his divine plan, "God ordains that what he hates will come to pass. It is not sin in God to will that there be sin."[23] He cannot be tempted by evil, nor does he tempt anyone else (Jam 1:13). "God is light, and in him is no darkness at all" (1 Jn 1:5b). The psalmist said, "Righteousness and justice are the foundation of your throne" (Ps 89:14a). God's work is perfect, his ways are just, and he is without sin (Deut 32:4). No one is holy like Yahweh (1 Sam 2:2).

The challenge is clear: the Bible expects us to believe several things simultaneously. If the Bible gives evidence that God decrees evil, then we should believe it. And if the Bible gives evidence that God himself is not evil, then we should believe that also. We may desire greater understanding in this area, but we must remember that

---

23   John Piper, "The Suffering of Christ and the Sovereignty of God," in *Suffering and the Sovereignty of God*, ed. John Piper and Justin Taylor (Wheaton: Crossway Books, 2006), 85.

there are secret things which belong only to the Lord (Deut 29:29).

It remains a mystery how God can ordain evil without being evil or being culpable for it, so we must preach to ourselves his transcendent wisdom. The Scripture asks, "For who has known the mind of the Lord, or who has been his counselor?" (Rom 11:34). God never acts unwisely in any of his decrees. We should echo Paul's words, "Oh, the depth of the riches and wisdom and knowledge of God! How unsearchable are his judgments and how inscrutable his ways!" (Rom 11:33).

Sinners are morally responsible and accountable. Even if we acknowledge God's transcendent wisdom, another objection surfaces: if God ordains sin without being morally responsible, why does he still hold sinners responsible for their sin? The answer is, God never sins when he ordains, but sinners always sin when they sin![24] Put another way, God is always blameless and sinners are always guilty, so he never lacks the authority or divine righteousness to judge sinners.

This truth is rooted in the worldview of the Bible, which proclaims a righteous God who will justly punish

---

24   D. A. Carson writes, "…God stands behind good and evil in somewhat different ways; that is, he stands behind good and evil *asymmetrically.* To put it bluntly, God stands behind evil in such a way that not even evil takes place outside the bounds of his sovereignty, yet the evil is not morally chargeable to him: it is always chargeable to secondary agents, to secondary causes" (*How Long, O Lord? Reflections on Suffering and Evil* , 2nd ed. [Grand Rapids: Baker Academic, 2006], 189). Therefore, I don't call God the "author" or "cause" of sin, since those words often denote culpability and participation in the evil deed.

evil. The psalmist warned the wicked, "But God will break you down forever; he will snatch and tear you from your tent; he will uproot you from the land of the living" (Ps 52:5). He "judges the world with righteousness" (Ps 9:8a). Vengeance belongs to God, and he will have the last word.

Faithful Bible characters saw no false dichotomy between his rule and his righteousness. God is absolutely sovereign, but his sovereignty never curtails or minimizes the moral responsibility of sinners.[25] In fact, "divine judgment presupposes human responsibility."[26]

But there is a further complexity. *If God decrees sin and suffering without being evil and then holds man responsible for wickedness, aren't we mere puppets?* Wayne Grudem rejects this inference: "In every case where we do evil, we know that we willingly choose to do it, and we realize that we are rightly to be blamed for it."[27] Paul taught that unbelievers indulge in fleshly passions and carry out the desires of their depraved minds (Eph 2:3).

Think back to the story of Joseph, where God and Joseph's brothers intended tragic events for different purposes. "The text will not allow the brothers to be classed as puppets and thus to escape their guilt."[28] The Bible

---

25 Carson, *How Long, O Lord?*, 179. Carson explains that these two truths comprise the view known as *compatibilism*—meaning, the two aforementioned truths are taught in the Bible and are mutually compatible.

26 Idem., *Divine Sovereignty and Human Responsibility: Biblical Perspectives in Tension* (Baker Books, 1994; Eugene: Wipf and Stock Publishers, 2002), 20.

27 Wayne Grudem, *Systematic Theology* (Grand Rapids: Zondervan, 1994), 329.

28 Carson, *Divine Sovereignty and Human Responsibility*, 10.

teaches that our choices are real. And in a depraved state sinners sometimes chose to do "what ought not to be done" (Rom 1:28).

God's Sovereignty is a Rock of Rest

God's comprehensive rule should ultimately stir faith, not frustration. I say *ultimately* because the biblical writers asked tough questions long before we did. They saw injustice and wondered about the purpose for the duration of evil. They were frustrated at times. They cried out to God, beat their chests, shed many tears, and endured much suffering.

The sovereignty of God was not an abstract doctrine to faithful followers—it kept them hopeful, it helped them persevere, and it can do the same for Christians now.

Kevin DeYoung helps explain the practicality of this doctrine: "There are no accidents in your life. Every economic downturn, every phone call in the middle of the night, every oncology report has been sent to us from the God who sees all things, plans all things, and loves us more than we know....God in His providence is for us and not against us."[29]

---

29   Kevin DeYoung, *The Good News We Almost Forgot: Rediscovering the Gospel in a 16th Century Catechism* (Chicago: Moody Publishers, 2010), 61.

Conclusion

In this chapter we have covered numerous biblical texts and anticipated objections to them. But truthfully we have only scratched the surface of how Christians in early and recent church history handled the problem of evil. The Bible doesn't tell us how God is able to ordain sin and suffering, hold us accountable for real choices, yet not be blamed himself.[30]

Nevertheless, we must believe several biblical truths at the same time: (1) God is sovereign over all sin, (2) man is responsible for his own iniquity, and (3) God is just and has authority to judge the wicked, since (4) the wicked sin according to their own evil desires.[31]

Don't let certain snares of philosophical logic keep you from embracing all that the Bible teaches about God's sovereignty. His ways are often mysterious, his thoughts are wiser than ours will ever be, his motives are always righteous, and his deeds are never wrong. He is good and does good.

---

30 Grudem, *Systematic Theology*, 330.
31 More wise words from Mark Talbot, "All the Good That Is Ours in Christ," 69-70: "We cannot understand how some human act can be fully explained in terms of God's having freely intended it without that explanation cancelling the freedom and responsibility of its human intenders. We cannot understand how divine and human agency are compatible in a way that allows the exercise of each kind of agency to be fully explanatory of some object or event.... Scripture reveals that both human agency and divine agency are to be fully affirmed without attempting to tell us how this can be, because we have no way to understand it, no matter what Scripture would say."

Our view of God's decrees should never incorporate divine culpability for sin and suffering. The wicked are responsible for wickedness, even though God is sovereign over both the sinner and the sin.

Despite its unusual syntax, reflect on this statement from the Westminster Confession of Faith:

> The almighty power, unsearchable wisdom, and infinite goodness of God so far manifest themselves in his providence, that it extendeth itself even to the first fall, and all other sins of angels and men...yet so, as the sinfulness thereof proceedeth only from the creature, and not from God, who being most holy and righteous, neither is nor can be the author or approver of sin.[32]

If the Bible guides believers to hold several truths simultaneously — which may at first seem contradictory — then we must submit our minds to his word and admit the element of mystery.

We can't fully articulate how God can be both three distinct yet indivisible persons and one divine being, but we believe in the trinity. We can't fully articulate how Jesus is both fully divine and fully human, but we believe in the incarnation of the Son of God. We can't fully articulate how the sinless Son of God bore the wrath of his Father for the iniquity of the world, but we believe in the propitiatory and substitutionary work of the cross.

---

32 Westminster Confession of Faith, Chapter 5, "On Divine Providence," Article IV.

We believe certain doctrines not because they're always explicable but because they're biblical. They may provoke questions or stir controversy, but hopefully such doctrines — particularly the sovereignty of God — will be an anchor for our souls and a reason for relentless trust in our all-wise God who does all things well.

3

The Worst Evil for the Greatest Good: The Sovereignty of God over the Cross

> Creation gazed upon His face;
> The ageless One in time's embrace
> Unveiled the Father's plan
> Of reconciling God and man.
>
> A second Adam walked the earth,
> Whose blameless life would break
>   the curse,
> Whose death would set us free
> To live with Him eternally.
>
> *From "Creation Sings the Father's Song"*
> *by Keith and Kristyn Getty*

The most terrible evil ever committed was the murder of Jesus on a cross, and God ordained every detail. He planned not merely the event of Jesus' death but also its manner of crucifixion, its timing, and the conspiracy leading up to it. At the cross, divine sovereignty and human responsibility intersect in an ultimate way.

This intersection prompts the tensions from the previous chapter: the Bible portrays God as good but the wicked as guilty, God as superintending the details but the wicked as eager participants, God as designing Jesus' death with good intentions but the wicked as designing it with evil hearts.

Since the cross prompts these tensions, this chapter can be thought of as a continuation of chapter 2. More than a specific instance of sin and suffering, the death of Jesus is the *pinnacle* of the evil that men can do according to the sovereign decree of God.

In two main sections, I will survey biblical texts which relate the tension between God's sovereignty and human responsibility to the cross. Then I will explain what the cross teaches about God's sovereignty over sin and suffering.

The Bible's Testimony of the Tension

The cross was the work of both God and man. To be precise, the biblical text teaches that wicked men succeeded against Jesus because their plans served the purpose of God. Perhaps Christopher Wright accurately summarizes your thoughts as he does mine: "I have to say at once that I don't understand this — in the sense that I can't hold both parts of it easily together in my head at the same time (God's sovereignty and human moral responsibility). Yet the Bible unquestionably affirms both. God acts through human actions — without turning people into puppets."[33]

First we will see the wickedness of the murderers, who were uncoerced and willingly carried out the conspiracy against Jesus. Then we will see God's sovereignty over the cross, since he not merely oversaw the act but predestined it.

The Cross and Human Wickedness

Jesus faced opposition from birth. The Gospels reveal conspiracy against Jesus from his infancy. Herod the Great feared the baby would threaten his throne (Matt 2:1-3), so he ordered the deaths of all male children in Bethlehem two years old or younger (2:16). By this decree he determined Jesus would surely be killed. Nevertheless, Jesus was protected (2:13-14, 20-21) and went to live in Nazareth (2:23).

As an adult, hostility surrounded Jesus throughout his public ministry. He was rejected in his hometown (Luke 4:24, 28), yet he continued to obey his Father. Jesus healed the sick and exorcised demons, and reports about him quickly spread to surrounding regions (4:31-41). Controversy followed him because of his bold actions, such as healing on the Sabbath (Mark 2:23-28). Because Jesus claimed authority to heal on such an occasion, the Jewish leaders sought to kill him (John 5:18).

---

33   Christopher J. H. Wright, *The God I Don't Understand: Reflections on Tough Questions of Faith* (Grand Rapids: Zondervan, 2008), 147.

While Jesus' works and ministry amazed many (Luke 4:36), his claims and actions provoked rising opposition. Eventually, his attendance of Jewish feasts incurred threats to his life (John 7:1-2). Jewish leaders weren't able to contain their conspiracy, and the people in Jerusalem spoke among themselves about the intentions of their leaders (7:25).

When attempts were made against Jesus, they were unsuccessful. He passed through the midst of some who tried to throw him down a cliff (Luke 4:30). Later, some sought to arrest him, but no one laid a hand on him (John 7:30). A group of Jews once tried to stone him for blasphemy, but Jesus hid himself and left the temple (8:59). On another occasion, Jews again prepared to stone him (10:31) and then to arrest him, but he escaped both their stones and their shackles (10:39).

After Jesus raised Lazarus from the dead, Jewish leaders gathered to determine how they would eliminate the threat Jesus posed to their political power and cherished position among the populace (John 11:47-48). "So from that day on they made plans to put him to death" (11:53).

Prompted by the devil, Judas Iscariot went to the Jewish leaders and agreed to betray Jesus for money (Luke 22:3-6; John 13:2). Accompanied by a band of soldiers and officers, Judas betrayed Jesus at the Garden of Gethsemane (John 18:1-3). Now that no onlooking crowd could object, the men arrested him (18:12).

Jesus was tried and crucified. The subsequent trials made a mockery of justice. At different points, Jesus stood before Annas, Caiaphas, Pilate, and Herod. Jewish leaders wanted Rome to condemn Jesus as an enemy of the state, so they accused him of insurrection. But when Jesus told Pilate that his kingdom was not of this world, Pilate told the Jews that the accused was innocent of political upheaval (John 18:33-38).

The Jews were not pleased, so Pilate commanded that Jesus be flogged (John 19:1). In a display of royal irony, soldiers pressed a crown of thorns onto his head and wrapped a purple robe around him (19:2). They mocked him with their words and struck him with their hands (19:3).

When Pilate again announced that he found Jesus not guilty, the leaders cried out, "Crucify him, crucify him!" (John 19:4-6). Against his better judgment and under the pressure of the raging crowd, Pilate delivered Jesus over to them (19:16). Barabbas, an *actual* insurrectionist, was released, and Jesus was condemned in his place (18:40). He was crucified on Golgotha, with criminals on each side (19:16-18).

Soldiers divided his garments and gambled for his tunic (John 19:23-24). His mother watched the horrible sight of her son stretched and displayed, covered in blood and closer to death with every passing minute (19:25). After he died (19:30), a soldier pierced his side with a spear, and blood and water flowed from the wound (19:34). The Jewish leaders had finally achieved what they desired.

The preceding record of the sins committed against Jesus confirms N. T. Wright's words, "...the death of Jesus is the point at which evil in all its forms has come rushing together."[34]

There has never been a more undeserving death than that of Jesus, who was tempted like men yet without sin (Heb 4:15). From the perspective of human compassion, his death was tragic, for he spoke wisely, healed the sick, connected with the ostracized, but died painfully as an alleged criminal. The cross was the worst evil ever committed by men.

But there is more to this story, another perspective to investigate — and it changes *everything*.

The Cross and Divine Sovereignty

The apostles preached a predestined cross. Before the resurrection, the disciples saw the crucifixion of Jesus as a defeat, a messianic disqualification. The resurrection, however, changed everything and gave them a message of messianic victory and vindication.

After Jesus ascended, the apostles proclaimed his death and resurrection. Peter unsurprisingly charged the Jewish leaders with the wrongful murder of Jesus, but he also described him as "delivered up according to the definite plan and foreknowledge of God" (Acts 2:23). Not delivered up despite God's plan but *according to* it.

While Peter's words persuasively tie God's sovereignty to the cross, most convincing is the prayer in Acts 4. The

---

34 N. T. Wright, *Evil and the Justice of God* (Downers Grove: IVP Books, 2006), 82-83.

believers addressed God as the "Sovereign Lord, who made the heaven and the earth and the sea and everything in them" (4:24). After this acknowledgment of his lordship as creator, they spoke about the conspiracy against Jesus, and it is important to consider their words in full: "for truly in this city there were gathered together against your holy servant Jesus, whom you anointed, both Herod and Pontius Pilate, along with the Gentiles and the peoples of Israel, *to do whatever your hand and your plan had predestined to take place*" (4:27-28).

This prayer testifies to God's perspective on the cross: his hand predestined the death of Jesus as well as all that led up to it. He guided every circumstance, every detail. But don't miss Peter's point: Herod, Pilate, and the Jews and Gentiles *did what they wanted to do* — kill Jesus — but unbeknownst to them they also carried out God's plan decreed before the foundation of the world (Rev 13:8; 1 Pet 1:20).[35]

If God, before creating anything, predestined that Jesus die on the cross for sinners, then the Fall of Man was also part of his plan. God didn't decree the fall because he approved of evil but because he wanted to display forever his grace and mercy to the redeemed (Rom 9:23; Eph 2:7; Gal 1:5).

---

35   I wrote a chapter entitled "The Gospel Planned Before All Creation: Why God Never Needed a Plan B" in my book *The Gospel is for Christians* (Brenham: Lucid Books, 2010). The chapter argues that it was always God's plan to send Jesus to the cross, not an alternative agenda implemented after Genesis 3.

In other words, God's wrath against sin highlights the glorious gift of his mercy to sinners. The first sin — and all subsequent sins — were part of God's precreation plan to display his mercy through the sacrifice of his Son. "Therefore, the biblical view is that the sufferings and death of Christ for sin are not planned after the actual sin of Adam but before."[36]

The Gospels teach a prophesied cross. It wasn't immediately clear — even to the disciples — that Jesus' death accomplished God's purpose. Peter rebuked Jesus when the latter said he must suffer and die (Mark 8:31-32). When Jesus rode a donkey into Jerusalem on the Sunday before Passover, his disciples didn't understand its significance; only in hindsight did things make sense (John 12:16). When Jesus washed the feet of his disciples (13:5), he symbolized the cleansing of his redemptive death (13:8), but they still didn't grasp the meaning until after his resurrection (13:7).

While they failed to comprehend the necessity of the cross, the disciples still heard Jesus teach that "the Son of Man must suffer many things and be rejected by the elders and the chief priests and the scribes and be killed, and after three days rise again" (Mark 8:31).

That he *must* be rejected points to divine necessity. Jesus told his disciples, "See, we are going up to Jerusalem, and everything that is written about the Son of Man by the prophets will be accomplished" (Luke 18:31). Jesus' death fulfilled Scripture, indicating that the cross was not

---

36   John Piper, *Spectacular Sins: And Their Global Purpose in the Glory of Christ* (Wheaton: Crossway, 2008), 59.

an entirely undisclosed event; there were prophecies to be fulfilled.

On a post-resurrection journey with two men, Jesus explained how the Old Testament pointed to himself (Luke 24:27). The expectation of a deliverer reaches back to the first book of the Bible. Before God expelled Adam and Eve from the Garden of Eden he promised the serpent, "I will put enmity between you and the woman, and between your offspring and her offspring; he shall bruise your head, and you shall bruise his heel" (Gen 3:15).

Jesus, the ultimate Seed of the woman, crushed the serpent by being crushed himself. The cross fulfilled the words of Isaiah 53:10a, "Yet it was the will of the LORD to crush him."

So, before the foundation of the world, God decreed the cross and the events surrounding it. In fulfillment of Scripture, Judas betrayed Jesus (John 13:18; 17:12), soldiers arrested Jesus (Matt 26:54, 56), a field was bought with the thirty pieces of silver which Judas had returned to the Jewish leaders (Matt 27:3, 8-10), soldiers cast lots for Jesus' tunic (John 19:24), the words of the psalmist found the fullest expression in Jesus' cry of abandonment (Matt 27:46), and Jesus died without any broken bones (John 19:36).

Even the timing of Jesus' passion was according to God's appointment, not man's. In John's Gospel, the terms *hour* and *time* referred to the anticipated event of glorification through crucifixion. Jesus spoke of his time or hour as "not yet" (e.g. John 2:4b; 7:6a), and the narrator wrote the same way (e.g. 7:30). When the cross was imminent, Jesus said, "The hour has come for the Son of Man to be glorified" (12:23; cf. 13:1; 16:32; 17:1).

Jesus couldn't be arrested, tried, or crucified before this hour had come, because God was completely sovereign over the timing of his Son's passion. No rash act of wicked men could precipitate the prophesied events before their appointed time.

God was sovereign over spiritual opposition to Jesus. So far we have seen how God was sovereign over the secondary causes of Jesus' death, causes which included Pilate, Herod, the Jewish leaders, and hostile Gentiles. But God's sovereignty extended further still. For example, demons played a role in Jesus' ministry, serving as foils for the authority and rule of the Light over the darkness.

Jesus once cast a demon from a man, and the crowd was amazed that evil spirits obeyed his command (Luke 4:35-36). On another occasion he rebuked a demon who possessed a boy, and those who watched the exorcism beheld the majesty of God (9:43). Demonic rebellion didn't nullify his rule.

God also exercised sovereignty over Satan during the ministry of Jesus. Satan tempted Jesus in the wilderness (Luke 4:2), only after the *Spirit* led Jesus there (4:1). Later, after Jesus sent out seventy-two people to proclaim the kingdom of God, they rejoiced when they subjected demons in his name (10:17). Jesus spoke about Satan's loss of authority, "I saw Satan fall like lightning from heaven. Behold, I have given you authority to tread on serpents and scorpions, and over all the power of the enemy, and nothing shall hurt you" (10:19). Satan could not victoriously oppose Jesus.

By focusing on several disciples, Satan heightened the repugnance of what Jesus endured. When Peter rebuked Jesus for teaching the necessity of suffering and death, he told Peter, "Get behind me, Satan! You are a hindrance to me. For you are not setting your mind on the things of God, but on the things of man" (Matt 16:21-23). Neither Peter nor Satan could dissuade Jesus from fulfilling God's plan.

During the week of the crucifixion, Satan entered into Judas Iscariot in order to carry out the betrayal of Jesus (Luke 22:3). But, as noted above, Judas's treachery fulfilled Scripture (John 13:18; 17:12). Although disloyalty by a trusted disciple is tragic, Satan's evil design only accomplished God's good design. God ordained the sin of betrayal as part of the means which sent Jesus to die for sins. And God's sovereign will operated in such a way that human responsibility was in no way mitigated; Judas was responsible even though used by Satan.[37]

Before Jesus was arrested, he told Peter, "Simon, Simon, behold, Satan demanded to have you, that he might sift you like wheat, but I have prayed for you that your faith may not fail" (Luke 22:31-32a). The prayer for Peter ensured that he did not ultimately abandon faith, despite

---

37   D. A. Carson, *Divine Sovereignty and Human Responsibility: Biblical Perspectives in Tension* (Grand Rapids: Baker Books, 1994; Eugene: Wipf and Stock, 2002), 132.

three denials. This story reminds me of Job, where God put Job in Satan's hand but limited what he could do to Job. In Luke 22, it appears that Peter was in Satan's hand, but both Peter and Satan were still in God's. Jesus prayed for Peter, and the Father heard his Son. Despite his malice, Satan cannot thwart the will of God. The Son's praying conquers Satan's preying.

God orchestrated the death of Jesus, and all secondary characters acted according to what he predestined to take place. Piper writes, "*Can it really be that God governs the sinful acts of men to make them serve his wise purposes without himself being a sinner?* Yes, he can. If he cannot, then there is no Christian gospel....There would be no gospel without the death of Christ. All the deeds that brought him to the cross were planned....And all those acts against Jesus were sin."[38]

Lessons from the Cross about Sin and Suffering

The remainder of this chapter will focus on two teachings which have other biblical support and center on the cross. The reason for keeping the cross central is this hope: if God ordained the worst evil to bring about the greatest good, then lesser evils are not beyond his decree or his ability to work good from them.

---

38   John Piper, *A Sweet and Bitter Providence: Sex, Race, and the Sovereignty of God* (Wheaton: Crossway, 2010), 115-16.

God's Will is Both Revealed and Concealed

God seems to will what he elsewhere prohibits. God is faithful, yet he decreed the betrayal of Jesus. God is truth, yet he ordained the false witnesses who accused Jesus at his trial. God is righteous, yet he predestined the injustices committed by Herod, Pilate, and the Jewish and Gentile opponents of Jesus. God prohibits the murder of the innocent, yet he designed the death of his blameless Son.

How do we explain these tensions in the text? One framework, or paradigm, for interpreting them is the notion of *two wills* in God: a secret will and a revealed will, also called his will of decree and his will of command. An advantage to this paradigm is its unashamed assertion that God can reveal in his law that murder is sin, yet he can mysteriously ordain the murder of Jesus without being evil himself.

This framework also argues that we are responsible to obey God's revealed will. We are accountable not to secret decrees but to his clear commands in Scripture. The Jewish leaders sinned when they murdered Jesus, because their actions violated God's revealed commands — yet their conspiracy against Jesus was according to God's will of decree. Put another way, "It is surpassingly sinful to reject, hate, abandon, betray, deny, condemn, spit upon, flog, mock, pierce, and kill the morally perfect, infinitely worthy, divine Son of God. And yet the Bible is explicit and clear that God himself planned these things."[39]

---

39   Idem., *Spectacular Sins*, 103.

This paradigm of God's two wills seeks to strike a balance between God's sovereignty (displayed in his secret will) and man's responsibility for choices (expressed in either obedience or disobedience to his revealed will). We need a framework that will hold these teachings of Scripture as simultaneously true, that will uphold God's control over his world, and that will validate the real choices that sinners make and are responsible for. This concept of a secret and revealed will of God endeavors to show that God is a righteous ruler and man is a guilty rebel.

Is a "two wills" model an imposition onto Scripture? But the two wills concept is not without criticism. Some have argued that it is an imposition onto Scripture. The critic might say, "Show me a verse that says God has a secret will and a revealed will, and I'll believe it. Until then, we shouldn't impose onto the text what isn't mentioned in the text."

This objection, though, will not stand under scrutiny. Although frameworks can be imposed unjustifiably onto the Bible, sometimes they are an attempt to describe what *is* there in the text. God commands us not to sin but then decrees what is sinful; he opposes evil yet designed the worst evil deed ever committed. Yet his sovereignty doesn't cancel our responsibility. Although God can ordain unrighteousness without compromising his righteousness, sinners always commit sin from unclean hearts (see Matt 15:18-20) are thus are responsible and unrighteous themselves.

What happens if we deny these nuances? We will inevitably downplay some part of the biblical witness. Instead we should acknowledge the complexity of God's will because we want to understand God's written revelation. The framework of the two wills, then, helps our minds try to grasp what the Bible conveys. And it conveys that God has sometimes secretly willed what he has otherwise revealed to be wrong.

Does a "two wills" model mean God is double-minded? Some contend that the two wills model portrays God as internally inconsistent. "This makes God divided," a guy once told me. But is that conclusion the only viable one? True, the two wills paradigm suggests that God both ordains and prohibits sin, but surely divine *complexity* rather than double-mindedness is the better explanation.

While critics are rightly concerned not to view the God of the Bible as double-minded, this concern only applies to a misperception of the paradigm. Those who teach that God has a will of decree and a will of command do *not* believe that God's nature is inconsistent. The distinction between a secret and revealed will doesn't imply a division within God. The terms capture the transcendence of God's ways.

When we look at God's revealed will, it forbids wickedness. So, when he ordains wickedness for his own purposes, there is obviously a secrecy to God's will that is inexplicable. This, again, is a case of God's ways being beyond our understanding. While some dislike an appeal to mystery, John Calvin asks, "Are you prepared to believe that nothing is lawful for God that you do not fully understand?"[40]

So despite some criticisms leveled against it, the framework should be retained as an historical effort to represent the nuances of God's will. "Those who reject God's revealed will fail to do justice to God's holiness, the majesty of the moral law, the seriousness of sin. Those, on the other hand, who deny God's secret will come into conflict with his omnipotence, wisdom, independence, and sovereignty."[41]

How can God delight in plans that include evil? One last question here. If God ordains evil yet is opposed to evil, how can God still delight in his plans? Wouldn't such a reaction expose God as delighting in evil?

Piper invites us to consider an illustration of *narrow and wide lenses*. God looks at tragedy and sin through a *narrow lens* and is appropriately grieved or angered, but when he looks at the same event through the *wide lens* of his goals in redemptive history he delights in the accomplishment of his will.[42]

Put another way, when God decrees disaster, he does not (through the narrow lens) delight in that tragedy or evil,

40   John Calvin, *The Secret Providence of God*, ed. Paul Helm (Wheaton: Crossway, 2010), 94.

41   Herman Bavinck, *God and Creation*, Reformed Dogmatics, vol. 2, ed. John Bolt and transl. John Vriend (Grand Rapids, Baker Academic, 2004), 245.

42   John Piper, *The Pleasures of God: Meditations on God's Delight in Being God* (Sisters: Multnomah, 2000), 336.

but insofar as the event displays his justice and furthers his plan to glorify his name in the world (a wide lens view) he is pleased with his decree.

For example, compare God's claim to take no pleasure in the death of the wicked (Ezek 18:23) with his delight in bringing ruin and destruction upon the Israelites (Deut 28:63). Or, in a similar sense, while the Lord wants all sinners to repent and not perish (2 Pet 3:9), John the Revelator records a summons that the people of God rejoice over the divine judgment exacted upon fallen Babylon (Rev 18:20).

God is not double-minded, nor is he temperamental. His thoughts and ways are transcendent, and his will(s) and emotions are complex.

Sin and Suffering Serve the Purposes of God

God rules with purpose. The Bible reveals a sovereign God who rules his world with intent, not randomness. Since God's rule encompasses all creation — good and evil — there is no such thing as a meaningless event. If something appears meaningless, remember we have a limited vantage point. Be mindful of who is where: we are on earth, God is in heaven (Eccl 5:2). He sees all, knows all, and governs all.

God's intentional rule is especially important when we consider the evil perpetrated against Jesus. Follow James Spiegel's reasoning about the cross:

The cross answers the problem of evil. The cross is the perfect example of God's wise yet mysterious ways. In God's infinite wisdom, evil will display the glory of his justice and righteousness. Paul taught that our unrighteousness shows the righteousness of God (Rom 3:5), but this truth doesn't give sinners a license for iniquity, because God is just when he condemns (Rom 3:8). In the cross, God predestined the unrighteousness of the hostile leaders so that his righteousness could be displayed (Rom 3:25-26). "People lift their hand to rebel against the Most High only to find that their rebellion is unwitting service in the wonderful designs of God."[45]

The murder of Jesus brought about the defeat of evil, the effects of which will be fully realized when Christ comes again to renew creation. So although the cross was—in an isolated sense—a horrific act of evil, it was also—in a greater way—God's declaration that evil will not go on unaccounted for. God the Creator is also the Judge, and the cross was his statement that evil deserves righteous wrath.

"The story of Gethsemane and of the crucifixion of Jesus of Nazareth present themselves in the New Testament as the strange, dark conclusion to the story of what God does about evil, of what happens to God's justice when it takes human flesh, when it gets its feet muddy in the garden and its hands bloody on the cross."[46]

---

45   Ibid., 35.
46   Wright, *Evil and the Justice of God*, 74.

God's purposes are often concealed. Knowing God has purposes for sin and suffering is not the same as knowing the *content* of those purposes. Take natural disasters as an example. We don't know God's intention(s) behind horrible events in the world, nor should we pretend to, but during catastrophes it never fails that some Christians quickly offer reasons why God judged the people who perished. Such statements can wrongly convey that those who perished deserved the judgment of God because they were worse sinners than those still alive.

Jesus corrected this faulty line of reasoning when he spoke about the eighteen people who were killed when the tower in Siloam fell. He asked, "Do you think that they were worse offenders than all the others who lived in Jerusalem? No, I tell you; but unless you repent, you will all likewise perish" (Luke 13:4-5).

In this life, there is no way to discern God's reasons behind tragic events—other than to simply say, "God is working all things according to the counsel of his will." A disaster doesn't occur because those who perished were necessarily worse sinners than the survivors. On the contrary, we all deserve the righteous judgment of God and should turn from our sins to him in genuine contrition and a heart full of faith in Jesus.

Still, God governs the events of the world according to his predetermined plan. Disaster and tragedy are no prevailing argument against God's existence and power. "That God cannot stop a germ or a car or a bullet or a demon is not good news; it is not the news of the Bible.

God can. And ten thousand times he does. But when he doesn't, he has his reasons."[47] We may not know these reasons in this life, but we must trust that he has them nonetheless.

Suffering serves Christian sanctification. For believers in particular, God sends suffering for good purposes. Trials test faith, which produce steadfastness and then maturity (Jam 1:2-4). Faith is more precious than gold and must be refined (1 Pet 1:7). Believers undergo discipline because they are his children (Heb 12:4-10).

God's good purposes mean that trials can come into our lives for different reasons, reasons not necessarily tied to any personal sin. For instance, Job was righteous when he faced the suffering narrated in Job 1 — 2. God described him as "blameless and upright" (1:8), but Job's friends *wrongly* assumed that his suffering was a consequence for sin (see the implicit accusation from Eliphaz in 4:7-9). Also, Jesus taught that a man's suffering isn't incontestably a result of transgression (John 9:1-3).

On the other hand, our sins *can* provoke the judgment of God in the form of physical suffering or death, and three examples can substantiate this. First, when Jesus healed a man who had been lame for thirty-eight years (John 5:5), he said, "Sin no more, that nothing worse may happen to you" (9:14). Second, when Ananias and Sapphira misrepresented the amount of money they brought to the apostles (Acts 5:1-2), God struck them down dead (5:5, 10).

---

47   Piper, *A Sweet and Bitter Providence*, 136-37.

And third, Paul explained to the Corinthians that receiving communion in an unworthy manner is "why many of you are weak and ill, and some have died" (1 Cor 11:30).

While the earthly suffering of unbelievers will culminate in their eternal suffering under God's wrath (2 Thess 1:8-9), believers have a different promise regarding our trials. We can trust that our "light momentary affliction is preparing for us an eternal weight of glory beyond all comparison" (2 Cor 4:17). When a Christian endures suffering with faith, God continues to cultivate Christlike character and hope (Rom 5:3-5), and our inward transformation will one day be joined by a glorified body (1 Cor 15:23; 2 Cor 5:1). Paul knew that when we share in the sufferings of Jesus, we will also one day attain the resurrection from the dead (Phil 3:10-11).

Because of the cross, believers can trust God to bring all sin and suffering into the service of his greater purposes. Paul expressed our hope in this memorable way, "And we know that for those who love God all things work together for good, for those who are called according to his purpose" (Rom 8:28).

All things include our sufferings and sorrows, temptations and sins. None of it is beyond his sovereignty, and he will work it all for our good, which—according to the next verse—refers to the consummation of his current work: conformance to the image of Christ (Rom 8:29).

Conclusion

Understanding how the Bible interprets the cross is central to how we can correctly (though incompletely) process God's sovereignty over evil. The cross shows that God ordained the worst evil for the greatest good, yet this design didn't coerce the opponents of Jesus to sin. They acted according to their desires and were culpable for their deeds. The cross reiterates the mystery discussed in chapter two: man is guilty and blameworthy, but God is merciful and praiseworthy.

The cross also supplies an answer to the problem of sin and suffering in the world. Piper writes,

> This was the moment — Good Friday — for which everything in the universe was planned. In conceiving a universe in which to display the glory of his grace, God did not choose plan B. There could be no greater display of the glory of the grace of God than what happened at Calvary. Everything leading to it and everything flowing from it is explained by it, including all the suffering in the world.[48]

So, before creation, the Father intended to send his Son into the world to live a righteous life and then die on a cross for the unrighteous. God made a way to forgive sinners without compromising his righteousness, so that

---

48   Idem., "The Suffering of Christ and the Sovereignty of God," in *Suffering and the Sovereignty of God*, ed. John Piper and Justin Taylor (Wheaton: Crossway Books, 2006), 82.

those who believe in Jesus could have their faith credited to them as righteousness and their sins no longer counted against them (Rom 4:3-8). This way, God is both just and justifier (Rom 3:26).

Since God planned and then redeemed the worst evil for the greatest good, we should trust that his control over all lesser evils will result in the accomplishment of his concealed purposes. God is not sinning when he ordains sin, nor does his decree compromise the moral responsibility of sinners. God is not divided or contrary in his nature; rather, he works all things according to the counsel of his perfect will, so that his glory and greatness will be displayed in all the earth.

4

The Rights and Righteousness of the Potter: The Sovereignty of God over Salvation and Judgment

"'Tis not that I did choose thee,
For, Lord, that could not be;
This heart would still refuse thee,
Hadst thou not chosen me.

Thou from the sin that stained me
Hast cleansed and set me free;
Of old thou hast ordained me,
That I should live to thee."

From "'Tis Not that I Did Choose Thee" by Josiah Condor

If the previous chapters can be compared to a short flight that braved some clouds of controversy, then this chapter adds turbulence. I hope my words are overstated, but believers can experience tremendous frustration when facing biblical texts about God's sovereignty over the salvation and judgment of sinners.

Any helpful book about God's sovereignty must address his roles as redeemer and judge, lest a major biblical theme be neglected. But I don't anticipate unanimous agreement on these matters, for few topics stir emotions among believers like the teaching of predestination.

By *predestination* I mean God's pre-creation choice to mercifully save some sinners from condemnation, meaning that the rest will be justly punished for their sins.[49] In other words, God rules over the salvation and judgment of sinners, determining who will receive mercy and who will receive justice.

The Biblical Evidence for the Predestination of Sinners

More than any other teaching about God's sovereignty, predestination troubled me most. I don't remember even thinking about it before college courses, but I remember my response when I heard that many people historically and presently affirmed this doctrine: I was disgusted. How could anyone believe God would do something so unfair,

---

49   This definition of predestination has a *Calvinistic* nuance, which emphasizes the unconditional nature of God's choice. In other words, no condition in sinners ever prompted God's choice of them for salvation. God didn't choose them because they were worthy, nor because he foresaw they would believe in Jesus. The basis of God's choice is his own act of free grace. It is also relevant to note that others in church history before John Calvin taught predestination this way.

something which violated man's free will, something that left the non-elect without a hope of ever being saved? Affirming predestination surely destroyed any motivation to pray for or evangelize unbelievers.

But here was my problem: as much as I didn't want it to be there, the word is in the Bible. More than that, other words communicate the same concept of God's unconditional act of saving grace. I wanted to just put my head in the sand, but pretending the concept wasn't there didn't make it go away. People have said to me in all seriousness, "The Bible doesn't teach predestination," but that statement — as good as it sounded at the time — couldn't be squared with texts that actually used the word!

John Stott wrote, "The doctrine of election is the product of divine revelation, not of human speculation. It was not invented by Calvin of Geneva or Augustine of Hippo. It is above all else a biblical doctrine and no biblical Christian can ignore it."[50]

The Bible speaks of God's initiative in salvation with words like *predestine, call, draw, elect, appoint,* and *choose.* These terms undeniably indicate that the Bible teaches predestination. So here's the million-dollar question: what does the Bible say *about* this doctrine? My answer is the same as a former seminary professor who dealt with the same subject: "Look at the text and tell me what it says." We will now do exactly that.

---

50   John Stott, *God's New Society* (Downers Grove: InterVarsity Press, 1982), 20.

A Chosen People

We must first see the truth of election applied to God's people in the Bible. The apostle Peter wrote to dispersed believers and called them "elect exiles" (1 Pet 1:1b), "a chosen race...a people for [God's] own possession" (2:9). The significance of these labels is great because Peter's readers included Gentiles. His readers were once "not a people, but now you are God's people; once you had not received mercy, but now you have received mercy" (2:10).

Election is the result of God's mercy shown to undeserving sinners. However, a lady once told me that everyone is predestined by God, and to become non-elect they have to reject Jesus and deliberately decide not to go to heaven.

Doesn't her comment reverse Peter's statement in 1 Peter 2:10? The apostle says once we were not God's people but now are, while her argument implies everyone was once part of God's true people but many of them now reject his saving decree have become non-elect. Nowhere in the Bible is this fancied notion taught. Before salvation we are under God's condemnation (John 3:18), and rejecting Christ only means we will remain under it.

Predestined Corporately and Individually

A college professor once told our class, "God has a corporate group of the Elect, and you must exercise your will to be a part of it." In other words, God creates a group that you can join if you want, sort of like someone who starts a new business and advertises that there are openings in the company — once you apply, you're hired. In this scenario, you become individually predestined *after* you believe.

But the Bible doesn't teach predestination that way. It's not a company we join, not a group we apply to, not an abstract entity with slots to be filled. The preceding verses from 1 Peter sound a strong corporate note (*God's people, elect exiles, chosen race*), but individual election is not excluded.

The apostle Paul is very clear regarding the timing of our election. He told the Ephesians that God "chose us in [Christ] before the foundation of the world....He predestined us for adoption as sons through Jesus Christ" (Eph 1:4-5). Before God made anything, he predestined sinners to be saved. The number of God's elect was divinely determined prior to creation. And this predestination was individual because it led to our adoption as sons.

Every believer is a child of God, adopted individually by him. And if we were *chosen* for this kind of adoption, then that election was individual as well.

One other piece of evidence highlights the individual component of divine election. Luke reports that after Paul preached the gospel to unbelievers at Pisidian Antioch, "as many as were appointed to eternal life believed" (Acts 13:48). Since true faith is expressed individually, those who believed did so because they were appointed individually by God for eternal life. Furthermore, *everyone* ("as many as") who was appointed believed, not some or most of God's elect there.

When God has appointed someone for salvation, they will at some point believe the gospel. They don't have the fictitious ability to reject God's predestination of them.

According to the Bible, believers are a chosen people, corporately and individually. We were once not his people, but then he showed us mercy, and mercy makes all the difference.

Predestined According to God's Will

Whose will is decisive in predestination? God predestined believers "according to the purpose of *his* will" (Eph 1:5) and "according to the purpose of *him* who works all things according to the counsel of *his* will" (1:11). Put another way, according to his will, God predestined some sinners to salvation. This decree was not random but purposeful, according to his pleasure and wisdom.

The primacy of God's will in predestination, however, does not eliminate the role of human response. Though their will is not determinative, sinners must repent and believe in order to be saved. Sinners will not repent and believe, however, unless God has first *chosen* them for salvation. Jesus claimed, "All that the Father gives me will come to me" (John 6:37a). But how do people come to Jesus? The Father must draw them by enabling their will to believe in the Savior (John 6:44, 65). God doesn't save sinners *against* their will. Rather, God draws them by enabling them to come, an enablement which changes the sinner's disposition. When God draws his elect, they *want* to come to him in faith.

Therefore, the sinner's desire is not the reason for God's election. He saved us "not because of our works but *because of his own purpose and grace*, which he gave us in Christ before the ages began" (2 Tim 1:9). Storms wrote, "I am persuaded that one reason Paul describes election as pre-temporal is to emphasize that the divine decision concerning human destiny is wholly unaffected by human deeds."[51] God's election is not based on what he foreknew sinners would do (Rom 9:11). God's free grace, not man's free will, is the ground of his decree (9:16).

By grace alone, according to his will alone, God wrote the names of his elect "in the book of life from the foundation of the world" (Rev 17:8).

Not Every Sinner Chosen for Salvation

While all sinners are unworthy of salvation, there is an inescapable implication: if God has mercifully chosen some for salvation, then others will remain justly condemned. In Paul's words, God has determined to harden some people for judgment rather than show mercy to them (Rom 9:18).

Consider just some of the many passages that demonstrate God's sovereignty over the judgment and unbelief of sinners:

---

51 Sam Storms, *Chosen for Life: The Case for Divine Election*, rev. ed. (Wheaton: Crossway Books, 2007), 107.

- God destroyed all people on earth except Noah and his family (Gen 7:21).
- God hardened pharaoh's heart so that the ruler would not free the Israelites (Exod 4:21).
- Moses spoke about gods which the Lord had allotted to the pagan nations (Deut 29:25-26), demonstrating his sovereignty over idolatry.
- God planned to destroy unrepentant Israelites (Isa 6:9-13).
- The writer of Proverbs said, "The LORD has made everything for its purpose, even the wicked for the day of trouble" (Prov 16:4).[52]
- Paul taught that God gave sinners over for more indulgence in wickedness (Rom 1:24, 26, 28).
- At the end-time judgment, if a sinner's name is not written in the book of life, God will cast that person into the lake of fire (Rev 20:15) for eternal destruction (2 Thess 1:9).

Predestined for a Purpose

The Bible speaks in different ways about God's purpose in election. He predestined us "to be conformed to the image of his Son" (Rom 8:29). God "chose us...that we should be holy and blameless before him" (Eph 1:4). He

---

52   D. A. Carson asks whether our conception of God is big enough to read Proverbs 16:4 "without secretly wishing the text could be excised from the Bible?" (*How Long, O Lord? Reflections on Suffering and Evil*, 2nd ed. [Grand Rapids: Baker Academic, 2006], 202).

"predestined us for adoption as sons through Jesus Christ" (1:5). In an ultimate sense, God elects people "to the praise of his glorious grace" (1:6).

The display of God's grace is crucial to his saving plan. God saves sinners "so that in the coming ages he might show the immeasurable riches of his grace in kindness toward us in Christ Jesus" (Eph 2:7). Put another way, his redemptive work eternally displays his unmerited favor.

Paul poses a related question: "What if God, desiring to show his wrath and to make known his power, has endured with much patience vessels of wrath prepared for destruction, *in order to make known the riches of his glory for vessels of mercy*, which he has prepared beforehand for glory?" (Rom 9:22-23).

God's everlasting wrath upon unbelievers proves the infinite value of his mercy. Through his decree to save sinners he showcases his glory and grace.

Praise for Predestination

Doxology, not controversy, is the point of election. He will never act unwisely or defame his name. Divine election serves God's overarching plan to display the weight of his glory and the wealth of his grace.

Paul praised God for the gracious election of sinners (Eph 1:3-4). God plans to make known the riches of his glory to vessels of mercy, not so that they will be indifferent to his grace but so that they will glorify him for it (Rom 9:23; Eph 1:6, 12). Elect believers from every nation will cry out, "Salvation belongs to our God who sits on the throne, and to the Lamb!" (Rev 7:9-10).

Adopting the Bible's Assumptions

When I first heard discussions about unconditional predestination, I became angry and frustrated because such an act seemed unfair. Over the last ten years this charge is the most common reason I've heard from people who reject unconditional election.

The argument might go like this: Doesn't everyone deserve a chance to be saved? And how can God be righteous in condemning those whom he hasn't predestined for salvation? Furthermore, if God has already chosen who will be saved, why should we pray for and evangelize unbelievers? Finally, what about the scores of biblical texts that command people to believe, repent, come to Jesus, or call upon God? Surely such passages, which strongly emphasize human responsibility, exclude any notion of unconditional election.

I approached the topic of predestination with a host of assumptions, and my approach seemed reasonable to me. If predestination were true, certain unbiblical implications seemed inevitable. Those implications (see the previous paragraph) seemed logical, which meant the cost to affirm unconditional election was simply too high.

But I continued to wrestle with the relevant texts, a struggle that went on for several years. No one was more surprised than me when I eventually concluded that the

Bible refuted my assumptions about predestination. It refuted them because it assumed some things of its own, things I'd not yet considered when studying the topic.

So, regarding unconditional divine election, what exactly does the *Bible* assume?

Sinners Deserve Judgment, Not Mercy

We are wrath-deserving rebels. Entitlement is the air we breathe, and it is toxic to our hearts and minds. Modern culture is dominated by the assertion of rights and the pursuit of "what I deserve," and this mindset has handicapped our thinking when it comes to the Bible. In a democracy we share our viewpoints, debate the wisest policies, and then cast our votes, but the Bible writers didn't announce a democracy.

They announced a kingdom—not just anyone's kingdom but the kingdom *of God*, an incumbent who will never be replaced. And in God's world he rules and does whatever pleases him (Ps 115:3). Under God's rule boastings of entitlements are laughable and dismissible, and the reason is crystal clear: though God created us in his image, we reject his rule (Rom 1:21) and go our own way (Isa 53:6).

Our entitlement, what we deserve, is judgment, not mercy. Rather than giving God wholehearted worship and thanksgiving, we revere created things and live ungratefully before our benevolent King (Rom 1:21-23).

We are rebels. From our hearts comes egregious wickedness (Matt 15:18-19). Our tongues deceive, our feet leave behind paths of ruin, and our eyes do not see the need to fear God (Rom 3:13, 16, 18). Our hearts are desperately sick, beyond any human cure (Jer 17:9).

As sinners rebelling against the righteous rule of our Creator, the whole world is accountable to God (Rom 3:19-20). Unbelievers are condemned because they hate light and love darkness (John 3:18-20) and live for the passions of their flesh (Eph 2:3; Rom 1:24, 26, 28). The deeds of men earn eternal punishment, not eternal life (Rom 6:23). Sinners can never merit his grace, for the only true entitlement is everlasting judgment in hell. The cumulative effect of all our works gains us nothing more than that.

Predestination is not unfair. God's mercy cannot be manipulated. No matter the ludicrous designs of men, he has no weakness to exploit. He cannot be bought, bullied, or bargained with. The one who dwells in inapproachable light is not intimidated by the ragings of foolish men. The Judge of the earth is righteous, so he will always do what is right (Gen 18:25).

Now the question is: what does this assumption — *sinners deserve judgment, not mercy* — have to do with unconditional predestination? The assumption nullifies the most common objection against the doctrine, namely, that God electing only some sinners to salvation is unfair. If everyone was in a spiritually neutral position, or if everyone was to one degree or another truly meriting God's grace, then the objection of unfairness could stick.

But let's keep this biblical truth in mind: nobody deserves God's favor, and everybody deserves his judgment. So for God to freely show mercy to some and not others is *not* an act of unfairness. The objector is wrongly assuming that if God predestines some he should predestine everyone.

The non-elect aren't people who should've been chosen but for some unknown reason weren't. Words like *ought* and *should* simply don't belong in a discussion about God's pre-creation predestination of some sinners for salvation.

When critics insist on the unfairness of unconditional election, they're approaching the issue without thinking through the implications of what we really deserve. Unfairness means someone should've acted differently. But since no one deserves election unto salvation, there's no unfairness when God shows mercy to some but not others.

Predestination Seems Objectionable

Paul anticipates the protest of injustice. Grasping human depravity is crucial to understanding predestination. Once we grasp that we deserve only judgment from God, it is clear that no one deserves salvation. Therefore, there is no unfairness when God shows mercy to some sinners but not others. Why isn't that unfair? Because, remember, fairness assumes words like *ought* and *should* (such as in the sentence, *He should show mercy to all*, or, *He ought to save everyone*).

However, "It is precisely this 'oughtness' that is foreign to the biblical concept of grace. Among the mass of fallen humanity, all guilty of sin before God and exposed to his justice, no one has any claim or entitlement to God's mercy."[53] So he is not unrighteous to show mercy to some and justice to others. His election is not conditioned by the will or deeds of the sinner. God doesn't predestine worthy people for salvation, nor does he harden innocent people for condemnation.

Nevertheless, Paul recognizes that predestination seems unjust. This concession should grant us all a sigh of relief, if only because we realize Paul isn't shouting through a megaphone, "Why on earth would you find this doctrine objectionable? I don't see how anyone could have a problem with what I'm teaching."

So if you — like I imagine is true for most Christians, at least initially — find predestination objectionable, just know the Bible assumes as much. But in Romans 9 Paul won't let you hold on to your objections very long.

Paul uses the stories of Isaac (Rom 9:7-9) and Jacob (9:10-13) to illustrate God's freedom in election, and he applies the principle of God's unconditional election to the subject of mercy and wrath (9:21-23).[54] Knowing his

---

53   R. C. Sproul, *What is Reformed Theology? Understanding the Basics* (Grand Rapids: Baker Books, 1997), 150.

54   For the argument that Romans 9 teaches the salvation of individuals, see Thomas R. Schreiner, "Does Romans 9 Teach Individual Election unto Salvation?" in *Still Sovereign* (Grand Rapids: Baker Books, 2000), 89-106. A defense of the same subject is John Piper's *The Justification of God: An Exegetical and Theological Study of Romans 9:1-23*, 2nd ed. (Grand Rapids: Baker, 1993), 56-73.

readers might object to his reasoning, he asks, "What shall we say then? Is there injustice on God's part?" (9:14).

Foreknown faith does not condition divine election. Paul's anticipated objection reveals that we correctly understand his argument. The logic of Romans 9 should *lead* to this kind of objection, the question about God's justice. Understanding why this objection would arise is vital to interpreting Paul's train of thought correctly!

If Paul wasn't asserting the unconditional divine election of some sinners to salvation, the anticipated objection makes no sense. After all, for many people the notion of conditional election doesn't seem objectionable! If a condition must be met to be God's elect, then we must meet it or we have no one to blame but ourselves for our exclusion from the Book of Life.

The argument in Romans 9, though, especially the first anticipated objection (9:14), excludes a commonly claimed condition for election. The claim is that divine predestination is based upon God's foreknowledge of a person's faith.[55]

God choosing those he knows will choose him? Seems to resonate with a sense of fairness, right? From a human

---

55   This interpretation coheres with one of the tenets of Arminianism. The Arminian view is named after Jacobus Arminius. Arminianism believes divine election is conditioned upon God's foreknowledge of the sinner's faith. This view, of course, strongly contrasts with the interpretation I've been advocated in this book: divine predestination is according to God's will alone, not taking anything into account (including what a sinner may or may not do). These two interpretations (the Arminian and the Calvinist) are the main historical views on the issue.

perspective it seems reasonable, and most objectors to unconditional election (at least those I've spoken with) have insisted on this *conditional* understanding. God looks into the future, sees who will use their will to believe in him, and he elects that person for eternal life.

Foreknowledge is mentioned is Romans 8:29, which is the chief textual basis for people arguing for election conditioned upon faith: "For those whom he foreknew he also predestined..." *What God foreknew*, it's sometimes argued, *is the sinner's faith, and on that basis he predestined.*

Note, though, that the verse never says God foreknew their faith. He foreknew *them* ("those whom"). To "know" someone beforehand has a rich Old Testament background of personal knowledge, not mere prescience.[56] Adam knew Eve in this way, and God knew Jeremiah likewise ("Before I formed you in the womb I *knew* you," Jer 1:5a).

In Romans 8:29 the "foreknowledge" most likely refers to God setting his saving, personal love on someone. Therefore God foreknew *people,* not their faith. Out of pure sovereign grace he set his love, his affections, on people whom he predestined unto salvation. Their faith was the eventual result of his prior administration of sovereign grace. Like 1 John 4:19 teaches, we love him because he first loved us, and this love was set upon us before he made the world.

Conditional election is neither biblical nor good news. There are two related problems with the belief that God

---

56   Michael Horton, *For Calvinism* (Grand Rapids: Zondervan, 2011), 58.

chooses those he foresees will choose him. First, this bases God's election on the will of sinners, a basis that explicitly contradicts Paul's argument in Romans 9. He insists that God's election does *not* take into account an individual's good or bad deeds ("not because of works," 9:11), nor does it depend on the human will ("not on human will or exertion," 9:16).

If Paul believed divine election was conditioned on the will of sinners, he could have said so; instead, he firmly rejects the human will as determining God's decision. Therefore, when people insist that predestination is based on God's foreknowledge of a sinner's faith, they are adopting a position that contradicts biblical teaching.

Second, if predestination to salvation depends on whether we first believe in Jesus, then none of us would ever be saved! This point is an implication of our inner condition. Spiritual depravity prevents sinners from initiating faith and repentance. Jesus said only those the Father "gave" to him would "come to/believe in" him (John 6:36-37). No one can believe unless they are first drawn by the Father (6:44). No one can seek God first (Rom 3:11b), nor can they love him first (1 John 4:19).

So, while election-based-upon-foreknown-faith may sound good and fair, it's actually terrible news. Since no one will ever initiate faith toward God without prior divine enablement to believe, God would be looking forever into the future for sinners who would trust him. He would only see rebels going their own way.

Paul anticipates the protest of God's right to judge. In Romans 9:19 Paul acknowledges a second possible objection to his teaching about unconditional divine election. This anticipated criticism further supports that unconditional predestination seems problematic, which, again, should put us at ease. Paul knows this isn't easy. He wants you to know, "I understand that if you're following my train of thought, you're likely to object here."

What criticism did Paul foresee this time? He asserted God's freedom to show mercy to whomever he chooses (Rom 9:18) and then said, "You will say to me then, 'Why does he still find fault? For who can resist his will?'" (9:19). Put another way, "Paul, if your teaching about divine election is true, then how can God judge unbelievers when he didn't predestine them for salvation?"

In the minds of some readers, Paul's teaching would seem to call into question God's righteous condemnation of the wicked. If the wicked are simply behaving according to God's will for them, in what reasonable sense are they blameworthy and can be judged justly? Unconditional divine election seems to remove any basis for holding unbelievers accountable on judgment day (Rom 9:19).

It'll take the whole next section to tackle that problem. Isn't it amazing, though, that Paul anticipated the objections of both ancient and modern-day readers?

God Possesses Sovereign Rights

God is free to show mercy. So far we have seen two biblical assumptions: first, sinners are entitled to nothing but God's judgment; second, from a human perspective, predestination seems objectionable in view of God's character and human responsibility.

Now we need to reflect on Paul's responses to his anticipated critics in Romans 9, and his answers can be distilled into a third biblical assumption: God possesses sovereign rights.

When Paul asked whether predestination implied injustice in God he answered, "By no means!" (Rom 9:14c). Paul then anchored his argument not in philosophical reasoning but in Scripture: "For [God] says to Moses, 'I will have mercy on whom I have mercy, and I will have compassion on whom I have compassion'" (Rom 9:15, citing Exod 33:19).

God's claim to Moses is reasserted through Paul to the readers of Romans: *God is sovereignly free to show mercy to whomever he wants.*

If people say God cannot justly show mercy to only some sinners, they deny God the very thing he claims to have: the freedom to bestow mercy at his discretion. God is not unrighteous to predestine some sinners for salvation, because he is not obligated to save any.

If God was obligated to save all sinners and then predestined only some, the charge of injustice would be legitimate. But who could make a biblical case that God is obligated to show mercy? In our sinful depravity we deserve nothing but wrath. If God had condemned us all, he would have been righteous. If instead he chooses some sinners for redemption, he is still righteous, for those who do not receive mercy will receive justice. According to Paul, God's unconditional election of some sinners to salvation is in accord with his righteous character.

Paul rebukes the objector for arrogance. The second objection to Paul's argument in Romans 9 pertains to human culpability: "Why does he still find fault? For who can resist his will?" (9:19).

Paul's answer is essentially, and perhaps surprisingly, a *rebuke*: "But who are you, O man, to answer back to God?" (Rom 9:20a). The objector has entered into the arena of back-talk. Only human arrogance leads sinners to accuse God of wrongly finding fault in them. So when the objector questions God, Paul questions the objector!

Paul fires more questions, continuing the interrogation with imaginary critics who haven't thought this issue through clearly. Like a good teacher he will help them. His next two questions evoke the image of a potter: "Will what is molded say to its molder, 'Why have you made me like this?' Has the potter no right over the clay, to make out of the same lump one vessel for honorable use and another for dishonorable use?" (Rom 9:20b-21).

Paul distills the debate down to the issue of God's prerogative. While clay has no right over its potter, the potter possesses rights over the clay. Humans "have no ultimate right to hold him accountable to our understanding of eternal things....It is he — not puny human creatures — who has the ultimate say in matters of eternal destinies."[57]

The implication is obvious: God is the Sovereign Potter who can do whatever he wants with whomever he wants.

Paul applies God's sovereign freedom to the subject of salvation and judgment: "So then [God] has mercy on whomever he wills, and he hardens whomever he wills" (Rom 9:18). As the Sovereign Potter, he prepares vessels of mercy for glory, as well as vessels of wrath for destruction (9:22-23).

R. C. Sproul said, "If we look closely at the text we will see that the clay with which the potter works is 'fallen' clay. One batch of clay receives mercy in order to become vessels of honor. That mercy presupposes a clay that is already guilty."[58] The Divine Potter molds sinful vessels while possessing sovereign rights over them and maintaining uncompromised righteousness in whatever he does with them.

Predestination Doesn't Nullify Prayer

The Bible's logic corrects human logic. Some critics of unconditional election say it makes praying for unbelievers pointless. "Why pray for people to be saved," so goes the objection, "when God has already predestined who will

---

57 Robert A. Peterson, *Election and Free Will: God's Gracious Choice and Our Responsibility*, Explorations in Biblical Theology, ed. Robert A. Peterson (Phillipsburg: P&R Publishing, 2007), 119.

58 R. C. Sproul, *Chosen By God* (Wheaton: Tyndale House Publishers, 1986), 153.

be saved?" Seems logical, right? The problem is this: the Bible never concludes that God's sovereignty invalidates prayer — a statement comprising our fourth biblical assumption.

While God has given us reason to use when reading Scripture, our reasoning remains affected by sin and needs to be (re)shaped by further exposure to Scripture. Sometimes logic seems to demand a conclusion that explicitly contradicts Scripture (e.g. *if unconditional election is true, then there's no point in praying for the lost*), and the mysterious intersection of sovereignty and prayer is a perfect example of this.

When our reasoning deviates from what the biblical text teaches, we should backtrack and unwaveringly affirm what the Bible teaches.

The writer of Romans 9 prayed for unbelievers. So what can be said to the critic who refuses to affirm both unconditional election and the call to pray for unbelievers to be saved? Once more the apostle Paul is our helper here, again in the letter to the Romans, and in the chapter *directly after* his argument about divine election and sovereign rights. Who knew the answer could be so close?

The opening words of Romans 10 are about Paul's petitionary posture toward unbelieving Jews: "Brothers, my heart's desire and *prayer to God for them is that they may be saved*" (10:1). Now either Paul was ignorant of the fact that Romans 9 contradicts Romans 10, or he believed divine unconditional election was theologically congruent with intercession for the souls of unbelievers.

Generally speaking, Paul's letters are filled with statements about prayer. He urged believers to pray that kings and political leaders would be saved (1 Tim 2:1-4). Paul commanded believers to "pray without ceasing" (1 Thess 5:17). In some of his letters he followed his opening salutation with a prayer for his readers (e.g. Eph 1:16-23; Col 1:9-14).

Therefore, while Paul held a comprehensive view of God's sovereignty (see Rom 11:36), he believed this doctrine was congruent with the practice of prayer in general and prayer for the lost in particular.

God ordains the means of prayer. If God commands prayer even though he has set some sinners apart for salvation, then he has ordained both the means *and* the end — prayer being the means toward the redemptive end. God delights to save his elect through the fervent prayers of his people. He is then doubly thanked and praised: for saving the lost, and for answering the intercession of his children.

Believers must hold to the biblical teachings about predestination and prayer, even though questions about each may remain unanswered. We don't know how many of our prayers have been ordained as God's means toward a saving end, and there's no way to find out. Our responsibility is not to speculate how much our praying "makes a difference" or "matters in the big picture." Are we to obey only after we figure out how much credit our prayers deserve? Our responsibility, as people of the kingdom, is to obey the King, so we should pray.

If God predestines some sinners for salvation, why should Christians pray for the salvation of unbelievers? Two sufficient reasons: the Bible commands it, and God ordains the means toward his appointed ends.

Predestination Doesn't Nullify Evangelism

God ordains the means of evangelism. Romans 10 explains the importance of proclaiming the gospel to unbelievers (10:14-15), an emphasis which serves as our fifth biblical assumption. Together, then, faithful praying and faithful evangelism are two means used by God to save his elect.

Paul's words and example sufficiently counter objectors who proclaim the uselessness of evangelism if unconditional election is true. Paul asserts that unbelievers cannot call on the Lord unless they believe in him, yet they cannot believe in someone of whom they are ignorant (Rom 10:14). So faithful evangelism is *necessary*, for God will save his elect through the only ordained means of salvation: believing in the true gospel of Jesus Christ.

Paul's example in Acts 18 shows his conviction of preaching to unbelievers so that the elect can be saved. When Paul experienced opposition in Corinth and prepared to leave (18:6), God told him in a dream, "Do not be afraid, but go on speaking and do not be silent, for I am with you, and no one will attack you to harm you, *for I have many in this city who are my people*" (18:9-10).

God promised to protect Paul's ministry because the city contained predestined sinners who needed to be reconciled with God. The divine command was to continue proclaiming the gospel so that God's elect could repent from their sins and trust in Jesus.

Charles Spurgeon believed election and evangelism go together, and so should we: "Because many are ordained to be caught, I spread my nets with eager expectation. I never could see why that should repress our zealous efforts. It seems to me to be the very thing that should awaken us with energy — that God has a people, and that these people shall be brought in."[59]

Predestination compels missional sacrifice. The truth of unconditional election motivated Paul to endure in the ministry, even amidst terrible suffering. Paul wrote to Timothy, "Therefore I endure everything for the sake of the elect, that they also may obtain the salvation that is in Christ Jesus with eternal glory" (2 Tim 2:10).

I want to make three observations about this verse. First, some of God's elect have not yet been saved, a reality that makes evangelism and missions crucial. Second, Paul's suffering was used by the Lord to take the gospel to the elect. Third, rather than compromising his passion for evangelism and missions, the doctrine of election actually motivated Paul to endure.

---

59 Charles Haddon Spurgeon, *Metropolitan Tabernacle Pulpit*, 63 vols. (Pasadena, TX: Pilgrim Publications, 1981), 26:622.

If the doctrine of predestination weakens your zeal for reaching the world with the gospel, then you have embraced false conclusions about God's sovereignty. "The problem, again, is that biblical truths are not being permitted to function in biblical ways. Inferences are being drawn from things truly taught in the Bible that are being used to disallow what the Bible clearly says elsewhere."[60]

If you hear someone insist, "You can't believe in God's unconditional election of sinners and still believe in evangelism and missions," don't accept such foolishness. We must hold to the complementary truths of the Bible, and it teaches that God will draw his elect from every nation through the faithful proclamation of the gospel of Jesus Christ.

Predestination Doesn't Nullify Obedience

God's elect are being sanctified. Someone might reason, *If unconditional election is true, then God's elect can live however they want and not lose their salvation.* Put another way, does predestination undermine biblical incentives to follow Jesus faithfully? No. I will show from the Bible that God's elect live for him, for he set them apart to be sinners transformed by grace. This brings us to our sixth and final biblical assumption about unconditional election: it doesn't nullify obedience to God.

When sinners repent and believe in Jesus, their salvation is both *already* and *not yet*. God declares believers

---

60   Carson, *How Long, O Lord?*, 210-11.

justified (Rom 8:1) and begins an ongoing inward work of the Spirit (2 Cor 4:16). And what God begins he will complete (Phil 1:6). We are saved, are being saved, and will be glorified (Rom 8:23, 30).

Believers must make their calling and election sure (2 Pet 1:10), and obeying that command involves growth in godliness (1:5-8). If a sinner doesn't desire to obey Jesus, that person has no biblical assurance of salvation (1 John 1:6; 2:4-6). "True Christians take very seriously their calling to reflect the holy character of the electing God."[61]

Election secures both salvation and obedience. Speaking frankly about his elect, Jesus said, "My sheep hear my voice, and I know them, and they follow me" (John 10:27). But not all sinners are sheep. Jesus told some Jews, "You do not believe because you are not part of my flock" (10:26). When Jesus calls his elect, they follow him.

In John 10:28 Jesus said, "I give them eternal life," which means the sheep are called sheep even before they're saved, "and they will never perish," which means spiritual death is not a possibility for God's elect, "and no one will snatch them out of my hand," which means they're secure from any assailant who would hope to damn any of God's people.

Sinners chosen for salvation are eternally secure in it, yet they will not live indifferently before the Lord who has shown them mercy. True disciples demonstrate true faith by abiding in Christ's word and holding to his teaching

---

61   Bruce Demarest, *The Cross and Salvation* (Wheaton: Crossway Books, 1997), 141.

(John 8:31). The Christian life is one of transformation into the likeness of Jesus, which fits with God's expressed purpose for predestination: he predestined sinners "to be conformed to the image of his Son" (Rom 8:29).

Predestination doesn't undermine the believer's responsibility to obey Jesus. God, who begins the good work of salvation in his elect (Phil 1:6), also "works in you, both to will and to work for his good pleasure" (2:13). Rather than compel believers to licentious behavior, "Belief in divine election...stimulates the believer's highest capacities to please and obey the Lord who has dealt with him so graciously."[62]

Conclusion

John Piper opens chapter 5 of *The Pleasures of God* like this:

> Can controversial teachings nurture Christlikeness? Before you answer this question, ask another one: Are there any significant biblical teachings that have not been controversial? I cannot think of even one, let alone the number we all need for the daily nurture of faith. If this is true, then we have no choice but to seek our food in the markets of controversy.... The teaching of Scripture on election has been controversial. But I believe with all my heart that it is precious beyond words and a great nourishment for the Christlikeness of faith.[63]

---

62 Ibid.
63 John Piper, *The Pleasures of God: Meditations on God's Delight in*

The previous sections seek to hold biblical teachings in their necessary tension: God is totally sovereign over salvation and judgment, yet sinners must repent and believe, or they will perish. God has chosen some sinners for salvation, yet his unconditional election never compromises his righteousness.

A biblical view of predestination affirms both divine rule and human responsibility. More than anything else the doctrine of predestination asserts God's sovereign freedom as the Potter who can do whatever he wants with whomever he wants.

Years ago when I wrestled with the teaching of divine election, only in hindsight did I realize a roadblock in my heart: I didn't *want* an electing God. I resisted the notion, looking for other compelling interpretations of certain texts. Then one day I was reading a textbook for one of my seminary classes, and my life was changed forever when I saw two specific sentences: "The problem is that we can't stand the idea of someone actually *above* us. We can't accept an electing God."[64]

Those may not be the most profound sentences you've ever laid eyes on, but rarely has my soul been so bared by something outside the Bible. That last sentence cut to the heart of the matter: *I didn't want an electing God.* I was

---

Being God (Sisters: Multnomah, 2000), 121.

64   Gerhard O. Forde, *On Being a Theologian of the Cross: Reflections on Luther's Heidelberg Disputation, 1518* (Grand Rapids: William B. Eerdmans Publishing Company, 1997), 52.

avoiding the conclusion to which the biblical evidence pointed. My assumptions were being challenged by biblical texts, but I struggled with relinquishing them. Yet if the Bible explains what it means for God to be sovereign over the salvation and judgment of sinners, then its conclusions are true regardless of what I want it to say.

Even after surveying the key texts and the common objections to unconditional divine election, perhaps you're still unconvinced it's what the Bible teaches. In that case I hope you will continue to engage the topic of predestination and ask the hard questions. Search the Scriptures, pray for wisdom and understanding, and talk with other believers about what you learn.

Let us rejoice over the truths of divine election and human responsibility in these words of Jesus, "All things have been handed over to me by my Father, and no one knows the Son except the Father, and no one knows the Father except the Son and anyone to whom the Son chooses to reveal him. Come to me, all who labor and are heavy laden, and I will give you rest" (Matt 11:27-28).

5

From Creation to Consummation: The Sovereignty of God over History and the Future

"Creation longs for His return,
When Christ shall reign upon the earth;
The bitter wars that rage
Are birth pains of a coming age.

When he renews the land and sky,
All heav'n will sing and earth reply
With one resplendent theme:
The glories of our God and King."

From "Creation Sings the Father's Song"
by Keith and Kristyn Getty

Like gazing around from a mountain top, in this final chapter we want to take in a panoramic view: God actively moves the course of history toward appointed purposes.

This activity is bound up with his identity: Jesus claimed to be the Alpha and Omega, the First and Last (Rev 1:17). From the beginning of creation to the climax and fulfillment of his plans, he rules.

Our God Who Acts With Unstoppable Purpose

> God the great Creator of all things doth uphold, direct, dispose, and govern all creatures, actions, and things, from the greatest even to the least, by his most wise and holy providence, according to his infallible foreknowledge, and the free and immutable counsel of his own will, to the praise of the glory of his wisdom, power, justice, goodness, and mercy.[65]

If the Bible teaches God's meticulous rule over all things for his glory and fame, then certain implications necessarily follow. First, God is more than a responder to events—he is actively moving, directing, and propelling history. Second, God has an overarching purpose toward which he is guiding all things. Third, no matter how fierce the opposition, God's will cannot be thwarted.

God Actively Plans, Ordains, and Directs

God is more than a spectator and responder. Some believers conceive of God primarily as a responder. He waits to see what we will do before he acts. He values human freedom and thus, like a "gentleman," stands

---

65   The Westminster Confession of Faith, Chapter 5, Article I.

politely out of the way until invited to intervene. What he wills depends on what humans will.

This common view of God renders him passive by default. The conception contains half-truths which make it subtly deceptive. The Bible certainly teaches that God answers prayer (John 14:13-14) and is a help in times of need (Ps 46:1), but a God-is-passive perspective is inadequate and flawed. Regarding prayer, for instance, John says that God grants our requests *if we pray according to the divine will* (1 John 5:14), indicating that *his* will, not ours, is primary.

The Bible insists that God actively works according to his purposes (Eph 1:11). From the opening words of Genesis, God acts, speaking into existence all things (1:1, 3). Boettner is right: "God is no mere spectator of the universe He has made, but is everywhere present and active, the all-sustaining ground, and all-governing power of all that is."[66]

God directs the course of history. The book of Isaiah is a great place to learn about God's sovereignty over history. The prophet says to God, "I will praise your name, for you have done wonderful things, plans formed of old, faithful and sure" (Isa 25:1b). Isaiah isn't exalting a God who merely reacts; he's worshiping Yahweh who forms plans and accomplishes them.

---

66   Loraine Boettner, *The Reformed Doctrine of Predestination* (Phillipsburg: Presbyterian and Reformed Publishing Company, 1932), 37.

For example, God planned to bring the Assyrians against the Israelites before the army's ruler, Sennacherib, ever conceived the attack: "Have you not heard that I *determined* it long ago? I *planned* from days of old what now I bring to pass, that you should make fortified cities crash into heaps of ruins" (Isa 37:26). God is accomplishing his agenda *through* Sennacherib.

God promised to deliver the Israelites from exile by prompting Cyrus the Persian king to permit their return (Isa 41:2a, 4). Isaiah reported God's claim: he "[declares] the end from the beginning and from ancient times things not yet done, saying, 'My counsel shall stand, and I will accomplish all my purpose.'....I have spoken, and I will bring it to pass; I have purposed, and I will do it" (Isa 46:10, 11b). His word accomplishes the purpose for which he sends it (Isa 55:11).

In Daniel 2, while the prophet was under the Babylonian rule of Nebuchadnezzar, God revealed to him the meaning of the king's dream. The dream was of a mighty statue whose different metals represented different empires (2:31-35), and Daniel proclaimed the truth of God's rule over them: "He changes times and seasons; he removes kings and sets up kings" (2:21). God dispenses earthly authority to whomever he wants, raising and bringing down kingdoms at his pleasure (Dan 4:17).

The previous passages from Isaiah and Daniel illustrate the truth of God's sovereignty over all historical events: he plans, ordains, and directs them. Yes, others make plans— just like Sennacherib and Cyrus and Nebuchadnezzar did—but their plans fulfill *God's*. This is his world, and he is operating in all things, propelling history with his wise hand.

Isaiah recognized that by fulfilling what he planned, God deserved praise for his wonderful works (Isa 25:1b). God decrees and then brings it to pass. Who is like our sovereign God?

God Plans and Acts with Purpose

The Bible describes different goals in God's plans, indicating his decrees aren't aimless or arbitrary. For instance, when God planned to free the captive Israelites through Cyrus, Isaiah recorded his words regarding the king: "I am the LORD, and there is no other, besides me there is no God; I equip you, though you do not know me, *that people may know…that there is none besides me*" (Isa 45:5-6). According to this divine disclosure, God showed his uniqueness and incomparability by appointing a pagan king to unwittingly serve his purposes.

God acted purposefully when he planned the death of his Son (a truth discussed in chapter 3). Through the cross and all it entailed, God planned the redemption of sinners. The opponents of Jesus fulfilled Scripture in their various roles, unknowingly accomplishing God's will (Acts 4:27-28).

God acts purposefully in the lives of believers. For them "all things work together for good" (Rom 8:28). This "good" is not primarily earthly comfort or ease, since the next verse speaks about being conformed to the image of Jesus (8:29). Believers can find comfort in the truth that he ordains and directs all events in their lives for their greatest good, something he alone can wisely discern.

God is purposefully directing history. He "works all things according to the counsel of his will" (Eph 1:11). And, in the previous verse, God has "a plan for the fullness of time, to unite all things in [Christ], things in heaven and things on earth" (1:10). Therefore, this climax is Christological in focus. Every knee will bow at the name of Jesus and confess that he is the world's true Lord (Phil 2:10-11).

God decrees and directs the unfolding events of this world for the fulfillment of this grand purpose: that "the earth will be filled with the knowledge of the glory of the LORD as the waters cover the sea" (Hab 2:14).

God's Purposeful Plans Cannot Be Thwarted

God is sovereign over his opposition. God reigns over those who resist him. He has faced opposition to his will beginning with the partial angelic rebellion. In the Garden of Eden mankind joined the resistance. Since that time worldly powers opposed the people of God as well. In the Old Testament Israel faced continual threats and eventual captivity. In the New Testament conspiring leaders demanded the death of Jesus. In the book of Acts Stephen was the first recorded martyr of the millions who would face his fate.

How should we understand such opposition in view of the Bible's teaching about God's sovereignty? We have seen that God designed the details of the cross before the foundation of the world. Since his plan was to send Jesus to die for sinners, sin must have been part of his plan as well. This means the angelic rebellion and the Fall of Man were part of his secret will. God didn't formulate his redemptive plan after the sinful actions of man but *before*.

Consider the opposition to Israel in the Old Testament. God raised up the Assyrians against the northern kingdom of Israel (Isa 37:26). He then raised up the Babylonians against the southern kingdom of Judah (Hab 1:6). After using these armies for his purposes God intended to judge them (Isa 37:29, 36-38; Hab 2:8, 16-17). He raised up Cyrus to permit the Jewish exiles to return to their land (Isa 45:5-6; 46:10-11; cf. 1 Kgs 12:15; Ezra 6:22). What does all this mean? All the opposition to Israel was according to God's plan.

Consider the opposition to the church. Jesus assured Peter of the church's triumph: "I will build my church, and the gates of hell shall not prevail against it" (Matt 16:18b). Persecution, then, doesn't mean that hell is prevailing against the church. When Christians face persecution for their faith, they are suffering according to God's will (1 Pet 4:19).

Paul taught his churches that Christians must enter God's kingdom through many tribulations (Acts 14:22). Concerning Paul in particular, Jesus told Ananias, "I will show him how much he must suffer for the sake of my name" (9:16). God will avenge his people, but not until the appointed number of martyrs has been completed (Rev 6:10-11) — a number *he* determined.

No one can stay God's hand. Despite the will and efforts of men, the purposes of God are unstoppable. Job said to God, "I know that you can do all things, and that *no purpose of yours can be thwarted*" (Job 42:2).

Nebuchadnezzar rightly recognized that "[God] does according to his will among the host of heaven and among the inhabitants of the earth; and *none can stay his hand* or say to him, 'What have you done?'" (Dan 4:35; cf. Isa 43:13). Piper reasons, "If a purpose of God came to naught, it would imply that there is a power greater than God's. It would imply that someone could stay His hand when He designs to do a thing."[67]

Consider political powers in general. When Paul commanded believers to be subject to governing authorities, he gave this reason: "For there is no authority except from God, and those that exist have been *instituted by God*" (Rom 13:1). Do you feel the weight of sovereignty in that statement? Paul called governments God's *servants* (13:4, 6). Regardless of their intent, they unknowingly accomplish God's purposes in the world.

When authorities exercise arrogant ambitions against God, it is rooted in their foolishness, but the nations will not accomplish anything contrary to God's secret will. The psalmist said, "The LORD brings the counsel of the nations to nothing; he frustrates the plans of the peoples" (Ps

---

67   John Piper, *Desiring God: Meditations of a Christian Hedonist* (Sister: Multnomah, 2003), 33.

33:10). If the Bible claims that worldly rulers cannot prevail against God's purposes, then we should gladly affirm that truth as well.

As I write these words, the world seems very unstable. America is at war, Egypt is in turmoil, Bahrain is experiencing degrees of violence and protest, and we still have ongoing concerns regarding countless other countries. The economy of the United States has much to be desired, and governments across the world are facing economic hardships of their own. And one problem that never fades is the global reality of continual opposition to the church. Though churches in Africa, Asia, and South America are experiencing waves of growth and revival, the work of the gospel is not without cost.

What does the Bible teach about God's sovereignty over these global matters of freedom, finances, and faith? Without exception, every earthly kingdom will be overcome, and the kingdom of the Ancient of Days will endure forever (Dan 2:44; 7:14). The world's entities are not independent of God's rule.

God's decrees prevail over his opposition. If you combined every nation of the world, they are only a drop of water in a bucket when compared to God's might and wisdom (Isa 40:15, 17). He "brings princes to nothing, and makes the rulers of the earth as emptiness" (40:23). Rulers may boast, but God needs only to blow on them and they will wither away into the wind (40:24).

When political powers actively oppose Christ's kingdom, God finds their vain efforts foolish. Many times he has seen the same scenario: "The kings of the earth set themselves and the rulers take counsel together, against the LORD and against his Anointed" (Ps 2:2). And his response? "He who sits in the heavens laughs; the Lord holds them in derision" (2:4).

Compared to God, the rulers of the earth are nothing. They are only in power because of his sovereign will. Their hearts are in his hand, and "he turns [them] wherever he will" (Prov 21:1). The psalmist declares God's global authority: "God reigns over the nations; God sits on his holy throne" (Ps 47:8). No evil alliance of spiritual and political forces can ever prevail against the decrees of God. While attempting to thwart his purposes, wicked rulers of the world will only fulfill them.

God propels the events of history toward their climactic conclusion. Ware asserts, "[God] controls the destiny of nations. He controls the outcome of history. Surely, the God of the Bible reigns as the sovereign ruler of all, accomplishing his will without failure, frustration, or defeat."[68]

The Hope of What is to Come

Aspects of the doctrine of God's sovereignty may remain controversial, but when the dust settles from debate and disagreement, believers should find their feet on a bedrock of hope, for God has the future in his hands. If

---

68 Bruce Ware, *God's Greater Glory: The Exalted God of Scripture and the Christian Faith* (Wheaton: Crossway Books, 2004), 77.

our good and wise God is sovereign, we can have hope, no matter how deep the sorrow, how fierce the storm, how great the battle.

The future is not dark and hopeless. Heed these words of Spurgeon: "Cheer up, Christian! Things are not left to chance: no blind fate rules the world. God hath purposes, and those purposes are fulfilled. God hath plans, and those plans are wise, and never can be dislocated."[69]

Through several magnificent events God will demonstrate his rule over the end of the world as we know it. Though scholars disagree over details of these happenings, evangelicals have adhered to this testimony of Christian orthodoxy throughout church history: God will raise both believers and unbelievers from the dead, he will judge unbelievers justly and eternally, and he will transform this present world into a new creation in which believers will dwell forever in fellowship with God and one another.

The Resurrection of the Dead

We are dying. Our bodies are prone to illness, weakness, harm, and death. Even young people who seem to have inexhaustible energy fall faint from weariness (Isa 40:30). Paul presents the sobering truth: the body is wasting away (2 Cor 4:16). This earthly vessel is a temporary tent (5:1),

---

69   Charles Haddon Spurgeon, *New Park Street Pulpit* (Pasadena, TX: Pilgrim Publications, 1981), 6:455.

but God has in store an eternal "house not made with hands" (5:1), a body that will one day clothe us (5:2, 4).

Believers will receive transformed physical bodies when the Lord Jesus returns, bodies that will forever display God's power over the last enemy (1 Cor 15:26). While Jesus' resurrection resulted in a glorified physical body (15:49; Phil 3:21), the enemy of death still enchains the unglorified physical bodies of the saints. Not until Jesus returns will the defeat of death be displayed by the act of resurrection and transformation (1 Cor 15:52, 54-55; cf. 1 Thess 4:15, 17).

Dust everywhere will one day be disturbed and unsettled. The returning Messiah will open his mouth and messianic tones of cosmic power will give the order of resurrection. Irresistibly, the dust will release the bodies that had returned to it. Imagine the explosive sight of molecules and matter standing at attention as transformed physical bodies take shape and shine brighter than the sun.

Christians should think often about their future bodily resurrection, for Paul considered it part of our "hope in God" (Acts 24:15). But what will happen to the bodies of unbelievers? Daniel heard this prediction: "And many of those who sleep in the dust of the earth shall awake, some to everlasting life, and some to shame and everlasting contempt" (Dan 12:2).

Jesus alluded to these words in Daniel when he said, "…an hour is coming when all who are in the tombs will hear [the Son of Man's] voice and come out, those who have done good to the resurrection of life, and those who have done evil to the resurrection of judgment" (John 5:28-29).

The sovereign voice of Jesus will cause physical resurrection: believers will be raised for life, and unbelievers will be raised for judgment. Holding to the Bible's teaching, Paul also believed in "a resurrection of both the just and the unjust" (Acts 24:15).

While Christians more often hear about their own resurrection at the trumpet sound, the Bible is clear: unbelievers will also exist eternally in a physical state, a state brought about by the voice of the reigning Christ when he returns to judge them. Let's turn to that subject now.

The Judgment of Unbelievers

When Paul stood before Governor Felix and spoke about the resurrection of believers and unbelievers, he categorized that future event as "a hope in God" (Acts 24:15). While we would certainly affirm that a glorified body is a tremendous hope for the Christian, why does Paul consider the resurrection of *unbelievers* part of this "hope in God"?

Believers should hope for the cosmic vindication of God's name which will occur when he condemns the wicked on judgment day. After God raises the dead, the unrighteous will face his justice and receive the full wages of their wickedness. This judgment displays God's righteousness and worth. On the last day evil does not get the last word.

God's sovereign judgment shows his rule over the destiny of unbelievers. They defy him in vain. It is common to hear people say, "God doesn't send anyone to hell — they send themselves," but this statement doesn't square with the biblical text. In Revelation 20 God judges the resurrected unbelievers (20:12-13) and throws them into the lake of fire (20:15). This place is the "eternal fire prepared for the devil and his angels" (Matt 25:41).

For now unbelievers may shake their fist at God, but he will crush them with the terror of his wrath. Paul describes the power of our sovereign Savior, who will be revealed on the last day "in flaming fire, inflicting vengeance on those who do not know God and on those who do not obey the gospel of our Lord Jesus. They will suffer the punishment of eternal destruction, away from the presence of the Lord and from the glory of his might" (2 Thess 1:8-9).

John received a vision depicting the horror of God's judgment. He heard the twenty-four elders say, "The nations raged, but your wrath came, and the time for the dead to be judged, and for...destroying the destroyers of the earth" (Rev 11:18). And the saints will shout, "Yes, Lord God the Almighty, true and just are your judgments!" (16:7).

All will see the righteousness of our sovereign God, and the saints will shout for joy. This is our hope.

The Renewal of Creation

While unbelievers will suffer under the everlasting justice of God, believers will experience the fullest expression of God's reign in the new creation. John reported this sight: "Then I saw a new heaven and a new earth, for the first heaven and the first earth had passed away, and the sea was no more" (Rev 21:1). Then the sovereign Lord, who sat upon the throne, said, "Behold, I am making all things new" (21:5a).

Believers who dwell in transformed bodies will inhabit a transformed world, for sinful "flesh and blood cannot inherit the kingdom of God, nor does the perishable inherit the imperishable" (1 Cor 15:50). So God will give us what we need for the new world: imperishable bodies for an imperishable kingdom.

Creation longs for this renewal. Currently God has subjected nature to futility (Rom 8:20), but its day of freedom will come. Believers groan for the redemption of their bodies (8:23), and creation is groaning for that day as well, when it obtains "the freedom of the glory of the children of God" (8:21-22).

God sovereignly subjected creation, and he will sovereignly transform it. He will eradicate the corruption of sin and fully reverse the curses of the fall. Peter pictures this transformation as a universal purification (2 Pet 3:10, 12). Because we believe God will accomplish this, "we are waiting for new heavens and a new earth in which righteousness dwells" (3:13).

In this new creation, believers will joyfully exalt their sovereign Creator and Redeemer. "From new moon to new moon, and from Sabbath to Sabbath, all flesh shall come to worship before me, declares the LORD" (Isa 66:23).

Conclusion

No one can compromise the purposes of God. He is sovereign over all spiritual and worldly opponents. Their hostility against him, their plotting and raging, is futile. God rules the rulers of the world, setting them up or bringing them down according to his will. He guides the course of history from creation to consummation, ensuring the fulfillment of his promises.

Since Christians can trust God's power to accomplish his will, they should be hopeful about the future. God will raise the righteous and the unrighteous. He will grant believers entrance into the fullness of the kingdom of life and will justly cast unbelievers into the lake of fire for everlasting judgment. He will purify the universe by eradicating the corruption of the Fall and by bringing together heaven and earth in a permanently renewed state.

The Bible teaches that God is sovereign over history and the future. From the first to the last, he is the First and Last, the Alpha and Omega.

Conclusion

From Him, Through Him, and To Him

"Absolute sovereignty is what I love to ascribe to God. But my first conviction was not so."[70] Many of us can identify with this statement from Jonathan Edwards. My own attitude toward the doctrine of God's sovereignty is different now than when my journey began ten years ago. Though I initially resisted the teaching and implications of the doctrine, I eventually embraced what the Bible was saying all along.

I agree with Kevin DeYoung's observation:

For many Christians, coming to grips with God's all-encompassing providence requires a massive shift in how they look at the world. It requires changing our vantage point—from seeing the cosmos as a place where man rules and God responds, to beholding a

---

70   Jonathan Edwards, "Personal Narrative," in *Jonathan Edwards: Representative Selections*, ed. C. H. Faust and T. H. Johnson (New York: Hill & Wang, 1962), 59.

universe where God creates and constantly controls with sovereign love and providential power.[71]

I have tried to show from the Bible that God's control and supreme rule in his world are clear from his own claims and integral to the worldview of the faithful saints in Scripture. The topics of this book, while only briefly treated, have engaged the most crucial aspects of this doctrine. He rules exhaustively and meticulously over the heavens and earth. He ordains all things good and evil, while mysteriously remaining untainted by evil and righteously holding wicked men accountable for their real choices. He designed the details of the cross so that he could bring the greatest good from the worst evil. He shows mercy at his pleasure, owing salvation to no one. He reigns over the past, and he is Lord over the future. He acts with purpose, and no one can thwart his decrees. This is our sovereign God, the God of the Bible, the God who *is*.

After reading this book, what is your heart's response? What effect should the doctrine of God's sovereignty have on believers?

Arthur Pink gives the right answer: "The becoming attitude for us to take is that of godly fear, implicit obedience, and unreserved resignation and submission. But not only so: the recognition of the sovereignty of God, and the realization that the Sovereign Himself is my *Father*,

---

71   Kevin DeYoung, *The Good News We Almost Forgot: Rediscovering the Gospel in a 16th Century Catechism* (Chicago: Moody Publishers, 2010), 60.

ought to overwhelm the heart and cause me to bow before Him in adoring worship."[72]

Beholding should lead to bowing. The sheer *Godness* of God should captivate us. Who but God is worthy of worship? Who but God should be praised forever because of who he is and what he has done? Who but God could declare that his own glory should fill the earth as the waters cover the sea? Who but God could fulfill all his promises and bring to pass all his decrees?

As was the case in Romans 11:36, when Paul contemplated the unsearchable depths and ways of our sovereign God, this doctrine should lead to doxology: "For from him and through him and to him are all things. To him be glory forever. Amen."

---

72   Arthur W. Pink, *The Sovereignty of God* (Grand Rapids: Baker Books, 1984), 190-91.

Bibliography

Bavinck, Herman. *God and Creation*. Reformed Dogmatics, vol. 2. Edited by John Bolt and translated by John Vriend. Grand Rapids, Baker Academic, 2004.

Boettner, Loraine. *The Reformed Doctrine of Predestination*. Phillipsburg: Presbyterian and Reformed Publishing Company, 1932.

Calvin, John. *The Secret Providence of God*. Edited by Paul Helm. Wheaton: Crossway, 2010.

Carson, D. A. *Divine Sovereignty and Human Responsibility: Biblical Perspectives in Tension*. Grand Rapids: Baker Books, 1994; Eugene: Wipf and Stock Publishers, 2002.

_____. *How Long, O Lord? Reflections on Suffering and Evil*. 2nd ed. Grand Rapids: Baker Academic, 2006.

Chase, Mitchell L. *The Gospel is for Christians*. Brenham: Lucid Books, 2010.

Demarest, Bruce. *The Cross and Salvation*. Wheaton: Crossway Books, 1997.

DeYoung, Kevin. *The Good News We Almost Forgot: Rediscovering the Gospel in a 16th Century Catechism.* Chicago: Moody Publishers, 2010.

Edwards, Jonathan. "Personal Narrative." In *Jonathan Edwards: Representative Selections.* Edited by C. H. Faust and T. H. Johnson. New York: Hill & Wang, 1962.

Erickson, Millard J. *Christian Theology.* 2nd ed. Grand Rapids: Baker Books, 1998.

Forde, Gerhard O. *On Being a Theological of the Cross: Reflections on Luther's Heidelberg Disputation, 1518.* Grand Rapids: William B. Eerdmans Publishing Company, 1997.

Frame, John M. *The Doctrine of God.* Phillipsburg: P&R, 2002.

_____. "The Problem of Evil." In *Suffering and the Goodness of God.* Theology in Community, ed. Christopher W. Morgan and Robert A. Peterson. Wheaton: Crossway Books, 2008.

Grudem, Wayne Grudem. *Systematic Theology.* Grand Rapids: Zondervan, 1994.

Horton, Michael. *For Calvinism.* Grand Rapids: Zondervan, 2011.

Lewis, Michael E. *A Theology of Suffering and Difficulty: Corporate and Personal Aspects*. Eugene: Wipf & Stock, 2006.

Merrill, Eugene. *Everlasting Dominion: A Theology of the Old Testament*. Nashville: B&H Publishing Group, 2006.

Peterson, Robert A. *Election and Free Will: God's Gracious Choice and Our Responsibility*. Explorations in Biblical Theology, ed. Robert A. Peterson. Phillipsburg: P&R Publishing, 2007.

Pink, Arthur W. *The Sovereignty of God*. Grand Rapids: Baker Books, 1984.

Piper, John. *Desiring God: Meditations of a Christian Hedonist*. Sisters: Multnomah, 2003.

_____. *The Justification of God: An Exegetical and Theological Study of Romans 9:1-23*. 2nd ed. Grand Rapids: Baker, 1993.

_____. *The Pleasures of God: Meditations on God's Delight in Being God*. Sisters: Multnomah, 2000.

_____. *Spectacular Sins: And Their Global Purpose in the Glory of Christ*. Wheaton: Crossway, 2008.

_____. "The Suffering of Christ and the Sovereignty of God." In *Suffering and the Sovereignty of God*, ed. John

Piper and Justin Taylor. Wheaton: Crossway Books, 2006.

_____. *A Sweet and Bitter Providence: Sex, Race, and the Sovereignty of God*. Wheaton: Crossway, 2010.

Schreiner, Thomas R. "Does Romans 9 Teach Individual Election unto Salvation?" In *Still Sovereign*. Grand Rapids: Baker Books, 2000.

Spiegel, James S. *The Benefits of Providence: A New Look at Divine Sovereignty*. Wheaton: Crossway Books, 2005.

Sproul, R. C. *Chosen By God*. Wheaton: Tyndale House Publishers, 1986.

_____. *What is Reformed Theology? Understanding the Basics*. Grand Rapids: Baker Books, 1997.

Spurgeon, Charles Haddon. *Metropolitan Tabernacle Pulpit*. 63 vols. Pasadena, TX: Pilgrim Publications, 1981.

_____. *New Park Street Pulpit*. Pasadena, TX: Pilgrim Publications, 1981.

Storms, Sam. *Chosen for Life: The Case for Divine Election*. Revised edition. Wheaton: Crossway Books, 2007.

Stott, John. *God's New Society*. Downers Grove: InterVarsity Press, 1982.

Talbot, Mark R. "All the Good That Is Ours in Christ." In *Suffering and the Sovereignty of God*, ed. John Piper and Justin Taylor. Wheaton: Crossway Books, 2006.

Waltke, Bruce K. *An Old Testament Theology: An Exegetical, Canonical, and Thematic Approach*. Grand Rapids: Zondervan, 2007.

Ware, Bruce A. *God's Greater Glory: The Exalted God of Scripture and the Christian Faith*. Wheaton: Crossway Books, 2004.

Wilson, N. D. *Notes from the Tilt-A-Whirl: Wide-Eyed Wonder in God's Spoken World*. Nashville: Thomas Nelson, 2009.

Wright, Christopher J. H. *The God I Don't Understand: Reflections on Tough Questions of Faith*. Grand Rapids: Zondervan, 2008.

Wright, N. T. *Evil and the Justice of God*. Downers Grove: IVP Books, 2006.

Acknowledgments

This book marks a ten-year milestone in a journey with an important doctrine: God's sovereignty. In a way, then, the last decade — and certainly the years before too — have prepared my heart for these five chapters. In God's kind providence, he steered my life into people who provided sound counsel, guidance, and encouragement down the rocky road of controversial truth.

I'm grateful to my wife Stacie, who believed in this project, and who over the years also walked this doctrinal path toward the same conclusions outlined in this book. She carefully read every draft I handed her, and her comments and red pen were valuable during the whole process. I began work on this manuscript when she was pregnant with our second son, and now that this book is published she is pregnant with our third. I like to think that writing a book is a kind of gestation. During my book's development I too experienced strange cravings, (mental) cramps and aches, and I looked forward to the day of delivery. You're reading these words because that day has arrived!

A heartfelt thanks must also go to Lucid Books, who accepted this manuscript and its topic with gladness and eagerness. I'm so grateful to Casey, Brad, Marissa, and the whole convergence of minds that help a book see the light of day.

Finally, *Behold Our Sovereign God* is dedicated to John Piper, and these few lines fall so short of what I feel when I think of how God has used him in my life. Other than the Bible, his sermons and books have instructed me more on God's sovereignty than all other things combined. He is a pastor-scholar in the truest sense. As his preaching pastorate at Bethlehem Baptist Church draws to a close, my heart is filled with thanksgiving for his faithful ministry and labor for God's glory.

Contact

I'm grateful, dear reader, that this book made its way (in God's providence no less!) into your hands. Thanks for reading.

If you have ministry needs related to the communication of the material in this book, or if you have general inquiries and comments about what I've shared, I can be contacted through my blog (mitchchase.wordpress.com) or more directly by email (mitchchase2005@gmail.com) or Twitter (@mitchellchase).

And if you're ever in Louisville, we'd love for you to join us when we gather for worship at Kosmosdale Baptist Church, where I have the privilege of serving as the Preaching Pastor.